The official companion to the documentary

Showrunners

The Art of Running a TV Show

The official companion to the documentary

Showrunners
The Art of Running a TV Show

TARA BENNETT

TITAN BOOKS

SHOWRUNNERS

Print edition ISBN: 9781783293575
E-book edition ISBN: 9781783297122

Published by Titan Books
A division of Titan Publishing Group Ltd
144 Southwark Street, London SE1 0UP

First edition: September 2014
1 3 5 7 9 10 8 6 4 2

A CIP catalogue record for this title is available from the British Library.

Printed and bound in the United States.

CONTENTS

FOREWORD

By Hart Hanson (Showrunner of *Bones, The Finder, Backstrom*)

One summer morning, a couple of years ago, I came to work on the Fox lot to find that a documentary crew was waiting to interview me for a film called *Showrunners*. I had no memory of agreeing to do any such thing (I still don't) but that is not odd for me. I agree to do things all the time—especially things that will happen more than two weeks in the future—because I know that day will never come.

But in this case the day had come and it was today. My intention was to blow them off. I had a rewrite to do on a *Bones* script, I was trying to get another Fox series called *The Finder* up and running, there was a sound mix, casting, and some sort of kerfuffle on set to do with how realistic a dead body looked—all in all a typical morning on a TV show for a showrunner and I hadn't even had my coffee.

The mistake I made was to speak to the documentary film crew in person and look the director, Des Doyle, in the eyes. Des has warm and intelligent eyes. Then he told me about his film, told me how hard he was working to make that film, and he convinced me that he was actually fascinated by the process of making "American TV." (Did I mention that Des and his crew are *Irish*? Like James Joyce Irish? Historically, these people survived a potato famine and the Troubles, so how the hell was I going to deny them because I hadn't had my coffee?)

I suspect all the other showrunners that Des Doyle spoke with fell into the same warm pit and decided to cooperate even though they too lacked the time and/or inclination.

Des convinced me that if I told him the truth about showrunning then the other showrunners might do the same thing. That was intriguing to me

because when it comes down to it, running an American TV show is like sex…
no matter how much you ask around or how many courses you attend there's
no real preparation for the real thing. And when it finally happens for real you
know in your heart that you're doing it in a maladroit manner. Tragically, even
years later, you may continue to believe that other people possess some secret
knowledge which allows them to perform at a much higher level than you do.
(Not just me. Other people too. Ask around.)

Another similarity between sex and showrunning (I have done both. Yes
I have.) is that when you actually do see someone else doing it, it's likely to
be accidental and traumatic such as catching your Uncle Buzzy in the tool
shed with the lady who cleans his teeth. (Not just me. Other people too.
Ask around.)

I know what you're thinking, "What about porn?" Let me tell you, porn
isn't necessarily a useful learning tool because porn results in self-loathing (*I
am not equipped like that*) and inappropriate moves that have no place in real
life (*what the hell did you do that for?*)

Well, thanks to Des Doyle and his committed group of Irish documentarian
filmmakers, you don't have to pick up your showrunning knowledge from
the street or Uncle Buzzy. What they've done is make a delightful, suitable-
for-work, non-pornographic film called *Showrunners*. This book is the official
companion to that film.

Showrunners tend to be an interesting group of people even if you aren't in
the TV business—probably because they are forced to live in two worlds: the
creative and the managerial. They must think equally with the left and right
hemispheres of their brains. The technical term for this is "schizophrenia."
Some are witty, some are cranky, some semi-catatonic. Most, but not all,
have terrible posture. Some are ineffably cool with tattoos while others are
inescapably dorky—some are both at the same time. And now you can see
them for yourself, in the film, and in this book.

Would you like to take a look behind closed doors? To get an inkling of
something that is usually private? That is not porn? Well, if it's between this

and Uncle Buzzy, then I heartily recommend the book and the movie. You may never watch TV the same way again.

Hart Hanson, Los Angeles, May 2014

INTRODUCTION

By Des Doyle (Writer & Director of *Showrunners*)

If you've just picked up this book in a store, or are reading the sample pages online, the rule of publishing states I need a killer opening line to grab your attention so here's my attempt—"It all started with Spock's brain!"

Yes, this book and the documentary film from whose loins it springs both happened as a result of me watching the 'Spock's Brain' episode of the original *Star Trek* series when I was about four years old. It's my earliest memory of watching a TV show and I think I found it rather scary (as many *Trek* fans do, albeit for other reasons) but it made me want to watch more of that show.

In my early childhood and teenage years growing up in Dublin, Ireland, the TV networks we mainly had access to—RTE (the Irish national broadcaster) and the BBC and ITV in the UK— were showing a huge amount of imported American TV drama and comedy series. I was reared on re-runs of *Star Trek*, *Battlestar Galactica*, *The A-Team*, *Knight Rider* (hmm, haven't these all been rebooted?) and long-lost classics such as *The Man From Atlantis* and *Automan* (someone please reboot them!).

These shows, all starring impossibly beautiful people and filmed in eternal, effervescent sunlight (it rains a lot in Ireland) with amazing special FX and stunts, made an indelible imprint on me. They were recognisably, profoundly different to the kinds of shows that either RTE, the BBC, or ITV were making at the time, partly due to the budgets involved but also the degree of ambition and imagination employed.

Later in life, my love for TV and film led me to studying film production and entering the business of filmmaking professionally, primarily as part of the camera department because that was the one part of the process that was essential to everything. You can make a film without anything except a camera—and being behind a camera meant you were always there at the moment of "birth," where all the director's ideas, the words on the page, and the actors' input melded into something new—something that had never existed before that moment, which was then immortalised.

After 12 years of working on all kinds of film, TV, and music projects with directors as diverse as Jim Sheridan, Barry Levinson, and Rob Bowman (yes, I asked him about *The X-Files*—a lot) I found myself getting a little creatively frustrated. Camera (unless you're the Director of Photography) is primarily a technical department and I wanted to explore something a little different.

Throughout those 12 years my love for TV, especially American TV shows, never diminished, and was fueled by a number of shows such as Chris Carter's *The X-Files* and Joss Whedon's *Buffy The Vampire Slayer*. As my love for those shows grew, so did my desire to know more about the people making them. I had been hearing and seeing a certain word bandied about in relation to the shows I loved and the people who made them, and that word was "showrunner." I became utterly fascinated with what exactly a showrunner was, and in particular, the people who were doing that job on my favorite shows, so I devoured every piece of information I could find about them.

In the 2000s I was watching David Chase's *The Sopranos*, Ron Moore's *Battlestar Galactica*, and David Milch's *Deadwood,* feeling like there was a real gear shift happening in terms of the amazing writing being done on these shows. And then there was the one that, in a way, changed my whole life: *Lost*.

In the film, when I interviewed Damon Lindelof (the co-creator and co-showrunner of *Lost*), he told me that meeting J.J. Abrams and making that show had completely changed his destiny. Well, for me, devotedly watching *Lost* changed mine, slowly, over the years.

When *Lost* literally crashed onto our screens there was a never-before-seen level of interest from fans around the world who watched the show for every piece of subtext, searching for every Easter Egg and looking for clues. They demanded more information about the show to such a degree that ABC, who produced the series, put its showrunners, Damon Lindelof and Carlton Cuse, out front and centre in the public eye to answer the fans because they were the only ones who really could.

This grew into podcasts, vodcasts, worldwide press interviews, appearances on late-night talk shows and even Damon and Carlton presenting specials about the show on ABC—the showrunners on *Lost* had become as famous and important to the show and the fans as the actors starring in it.

With the continuing growth of the Internet and the arrival of social media, this level of fan devotion spread across a ton of shows. Suddenly these showrunners were in direct contact with their fans, and yet every day I would read comments and postings from fans who either didn't understand what a showrunner did, or were badly misinformed about the job.

I waited diligently for a documentary to come along to explain to everyone exactly what a showrunner was and the intricacies of their job, but it never did. And that's when I had that crazy, life-changing idea—well, maybe I could make one.

Cut to four years later and the film is finally finished and there's also this official companion book which you're reading right now (you kept reading, didn't you?). The making of the *Showrunners* documentary has been the most difficult and challenging thing I have ever done, and the most rewarding. It has provided me with the opportunity to meet many of my heroes, and indeed, many of them are in the film. I've been given the chance to spend time in writers' rooms on shows and watch that creative process unfold. We spent time on sets with the showrunners, watching them interact with their cast and crews, and even directing episodes of their shows. We were in editing suites with them, in production meetings, on red carpets, and in press rooms. We were given a VIP pass into the world of the showrunner, and I still can't quite believe that happened. But it did, and I am very, very grateful for it.

If you've seen the film, you hopefully now understand their world a lot better. But as with all films, we couldn't include everything in 90 minutes, and that is where this wonderful book comes in. Inside we've been able to go a little deeper, as well as include exclusive contributions from some gifted showrunners that we very unfortunately could not include in the film for various reasons.

All of the showrunners provide a great deal of wisdom and insight about what it takes to create, write, produce, and deliver a TV show in the current universe of broadcasting, as well as some thoughts on how to become a showrunner in the first place. For every showrunner it's a fight to get on the air and then to stay on the air. They are remarkable people. And this is an expansion of our cinematic foray into their stories.

To all of the actors, writers, editors, producers, and network presidents who allowed us to be a part of their world for a little while—thank you so much! To everyone who helped me make the film—and there were so many amazing people who contributed to it—my heartfelt thanks. To the people who funded the film, both the Irish Film Board and our Kickstarter backers, thank you for believing in us! Thanks to my family for their tireless support of me and to my friends who have remained my friends despite not seeing me for the best part of four years! My thanks also to Titan Books and Tara Bennett for wanting to do this book—that's two off my bucket list now!

Thanks also to the impossibly likeable Hart Hanson for providing us with a foreword and saying nice things about my eyes. To everyone who has watched the film or who has bought this book—thank you for your interest, I sincerely hope you enjoy it.

And last but most definitely not least—to every showrunner who took part in the film and the book, you have my eternal gratitude. I still can't believe how kind and generous you have all been to us. I hope the book and film meet with your approval. After asking so many favors of you all for so long, I'm amazed that all of you still respond to my emails. Maybe it's because you know I'm a genuine fan of what you do.

Des Doyle
Dublin, Ireland, May 2014

CHAPTER ONE

DEFINITION OF A SHOWRUNNER

BIRTH OF THE SHOWRUNNER

Television. For the better part of six decades, it was the square box that commanded our evening's attention. Then it became the thin rectangle. Now television doesn't have dimensions anymore, as our phones, tablets, and monitors are the conduits to our entertainment. As technology has whisked a generation of viewing habits away in a mere decade, so too has the content we watch outgrown the mundane labels of plain old sitcom and drama.

Scripted television content in the late 1940s came out of the gate with a flood of quality, ushering in the first "Golden Age" of teleplays, dramas, and episodic stories. In that era, viewers got lost in the novelty of the personalized melodrama, the actors, the dramatic tension, or comedic feats. But by program's end, the box was powered down without viewers lingering much on the names who crafted the stories that captivated their imaginations.

As television evolved, great heights of storytelling were achieved from *Roots* to *Star Trek*, but we can all admit, a whole lot of mediocre material cropped up too. A vast percentage of programming leaned towards the comfort-food spectrum of entertainment, or providing vehicles for entertainers to become household names. Concentrated blocks of mesmerizing, scripted quality had its peak in the past.

Fast-forward to the age of the Internet and the subsequent sea-change in viewer awareness. As the 1990s came to a close, another box was vying for entertainment attention as millions were discovering that the computer was a conduit to carry on the television discussion after the fade to black. Digital communities formed around television shows. With immediate mass connectivity, it wasn't enough to discuss what was seen the next morning around the proverbial watercooler. The conversation couldn't, and didn't have to, wait anymore.

Dissecting plot twists, performances, characters' romantic entanglements, and infuriating turning points became a pastime for scripted-television connoisseurs, whether it was on boards like Television Without Pity or private news lists that evolved into community hubs for beloved shows. And with this new pastime came the unexpected "outing" of the names in the credits who were responsible for drafting the stories that engendered such audience obsession.

Granted, there have always been those who hailed the brilliant minds behind the scripts, especially critics, but Internet attention smashed open the gates of adulation so it wasn't just the lead actors who gained the praise for a show's success. Now, the brains behind the series concepts—the David Chases, Joss Whedons, and J.J. Abramses—were being referenced with the same kind of star-struck reverence as any sparkling leading man or woman.

Who would have ever bought that the pale, weary, self-deprecating talents plunking tirelessly on their abused keyboards would become the pin-up faces for the modern era's latest Golden Age of television? No writer would ever delude themselves that that bizarro pitch would get picked up, but picked up it has by audiences who have run with it to make television creators as beloved and name-checked as their cast.

The awareness of the job has even birthed a new term to define it into the pop culture lexicon: the showrunner.

A few years ago, that word would have garnered confused looks by those outside of the industry. Instead it's gaining more and more traction, with every Internet article that TV aficionados read detailing the development plans of popular show creators, or season finale post-mortem features that grill a showrunner on the micro-choices made drafting a season. *Showrunners* is even the title of the documentary for which this book serves as the official companion guide, and it certainly doesn't get bigger than this (as we'd like to think).

SHOWRUNNER 101

Pedantically, the Oxford Dictionary defines a "showrunner" as "The person who has overall creative authority and management responsibility for a television program." Writers' Guild of America (WGA) members (the labor union for film and television writers) have known that job to be the executive producer position since the guild started arbitrating writing credits titles back in 1941.

In practice, the showrunner is the big brain of an episodic television series, and the executor of the ordered number of scripts for a given season. But what does that mean day-to-day to a person sitting at the helm?

As it turns out, the specifics of the job are consistent, yet very individual to a person's particular focus. How they each define the job is telling about their priorities within the position and how they execute the post.

JEFF PINKNER, SHOWRUNNER: ALIAS, FRINGE

I think the term "showrunner" is a fairly recent term of art. There have been TV shows for a long time. TV shows are, at the end of the day, fairly militaristic in that somebody's at the head making choices and, unlike features, in television it's typically a writer-producer who is looking out not only for the scripts, not only for the storytelling, but ultimately for the cuts that go out on the air, overseeing production as well.

It's a lot to manage. It used to be that television shows were simpler. Television shows now are very cinematic. The production value is much higher. It's not a stage-bound show. There are days on stage, but then there are also days on location. The management of a television show has gotten much, much harder and yet every seven days one goes on the air.

ANDREW MARLOWE, SHOWRUNNER: CASTLE

Being the showrunner means that you're responsible for all the creative and financial aspects of the show. You're responsible for taking an idea of the show, an idea for each episode, all the way through execution, all the way to a physical deliverable that you're giving to the network that they're going to be broadcasting over air. It's like being a CEO of an organization, where a typical budget is $2.8m to $3.5m an episode. At the end of the year, you've been the CEO of an endeavor that is a $70m to $75m endeavor. So it is being responsible for that organization, from top to bottom, and making sure that it runs smoothly and making sure that it delivers a really great product for the folks that you're working for, folks that are investing in you.

HART HANSON, SHOWRUNNER: BONES, THE FINDER, BACKSTROM

We showrunners used to be fairly anonymous, which seems to me to be better. Then there were people—long before I got into TV—like David E. Kelley or Steven Bochco, David Milch, that you knew of. Tom Fontana was the first showrunner where I realized, "Oh man, every time this guy does a show, I think it's wonderful." Now, there's tons of us that at least our audiences seem to know, or a portion of our audiences seem to know. It's a strange development. I think there's in-front-of-the-camera people, and I think there's behind-the-camera people. I guess there are a few people who are good on either side. You kind of choose to be behind the camera so that you can have that kind of life.

DAMON LINDELOF, SHOWRUNNER: LOST, THE LEFTOVERS

I think the Internet had to exist in order to create the story of the showrunner, the rise of the showrunner as you call it. I think that because *Lost* was what it was and because the writing itself became this thing that a lot of people were curious about—who is making up this story, we are really interested in the story itself—you have to be a serialized storyteller in order to do so. Can you imagine if David Lynch had an interest in and access to the Internet when *Twin Peaks* came along? I think that with what happened with Carlton (Cuse) and I, David

Lynch absolutely would have been on talk shows, communicating directly with his fans. People would have known much more, there would have been a greater sense of authorship there.

JOSS WHEDON, SHOWRUNNER: BUFFY THE VAMPIRE SLAYER, FIREFLY, DOLLHOUSE

I loved being a showrunner. It was the first time in my career that anybody paid attention to me. That was nice. But, also, I was surrounded by extraordinarily talented people and we were all on the same mission. To do that, whether you're fighting with a network or they're loving every minute of it, you have this enormous bond. It's a feeling you don't get from the movies because there everybody meets, does their thing, and goes their separate ways. On a TV show, for better or for worse, you're stuck together, unless I fire you. It creates something that becomes more than the sum of its parts.

JAMES DUFF, SHOWRUNNER: THE CLOSER, MAJOR CRIMES

Everyone who does this job defines for themselves what it means. Doing a job like this, running a show, when you are breaking a story, say, for episode 11, doing an edit on episode one, doing a mix perhaps on episode two, writing yourself episode seven, and trying to cast episode six while episode five is shooting, I mean, it's crazy. You would look at that and think, "Nobody can do all this," and you would be right. You need to know where you ought to be and then you have to be there. That's just part of your figuring out what your job is, I think. You can be pulled in a thousand different directions.

JANE ESPENSON, SHOWRUNNER: CAPRICA, HUSBANDS

A showrunner has to have a bit of dictator in them and has to be able to say, "Yeah, I know you don't think you quite have enough work with it. I know you're not happy. Deal with it." You have to be willing to piss people off, willing to make the unpopular decision. I think it's a job that requires a lot of toughness. I think it requires a willingness to offend because you've got to see the people that are standing between you and your vision.

ALI LeROI, Showrunner: Everybody Hates Chris, Are We There Yet?

The job of a showrunner? You come in wanting to be creative, but you end up directing traffic. Sounds glossy, but really it's a billion decisions a day. You're the guy that has to decide what we're going to do. You're the guy that has to decide how the problem is going to be solved. They only bring you questions, and hopefully you have the right answers.

If people respond to it in millions of numbers positively, then your answers are good. If they don't, then your answers are bad. Even as a showrunner, it's not your creative vision that is the one that endures, it's the administrative one. If the decisions you're making make the products successful, then they're happy with you. They don't care how creative you are. They'll fire the showrunner and they'll hire another showrunner because what they want is for the thing that they bankrolled to be successful.

Even if you came up with the idea for what you think the perfect sandwich is, if you slap some condiments on that don't make any sense to them, they go, "No, no, no, no, no! We like the bread and the meat but let's try something else on top, and that guy wants to put mustard on everything. So, let's get rid of him and get a guy who'll put on there what we say to put on there, and maybe that'll work." You problem-solve, you direct traffic, you delegate, and every now and again you try and come up with something that you think is a good idea.

KURT SUTTER, Showrunner: Sons of Anarchy

As difficult and as time-consuming and as stressful as it can be, I mean creatively, to be able to tell these stories and have the control over it that I do is such a rare thing. The great thing about TV is you can have the idea on Monday, write it on Tuesday, film it on Wednesday, and watch it on Friday, and there's very few mediums out there that allow you to do that. I'm a writer who loves to write, and I know that sounds obvious, but there are a lot of people who are great writers who really don't necessarily enjoy the process, and I really do. I love the first draft as much as I love the rewrites. The idea of really having those characters come alive in my head and hearing the words is just… it's a rush for me, and I also love the post-process. Post for me is the final draft, and you can really go in and shape and finish telling the story in post.

MATTHEW CARNAHAN, Showrunner: House of Lies

I don't know if I love being a showrunner on its own. I love getting to tell a story in a big novelistic way, that's what I love. The thrill of showrunning, of having a lot of people staring at you and wondering what to do, is not . . .that's not the thing that does it for me, but having a bunch of talented writers and being able to help tell a story is extremely satisfying.

I think between casting the next episode, being on set for the episode you're shooting, being in the writers' room, dealing with budgets and everything, I would say that showrunning is as much a feat of choreography as it is of anything else. It's really, "How am I going to parse my day into 300 tiny parts and be present for any of them?" Showrunning has this slightly, almost glamorous patina to it. For me, a lot of it is the grind of selling the show, pitching the show, getting it sold, getting your deal made, getting an outline approved. These are the most mundane, banal tasks you can imagine, especially the bigger network version of that. And then there's all the grinding out of the actual script, which is what it is. The nice thing about all of that writing and pitching and writing some more and pitching some more and then going through the process and then going into production and post, is that it's the reason they let me do any of the stuff that I do, and that I can write okay. And you get to go from periods of total introversion to total extroversion. I could not handle just extroversion. There's no way. Getting to go from one to another and then back into your cave and write some more, it's a nice ebb and flow. That, to me, is the best thing about it.

MIKE ROYCE, Showrunner: Men of a Certain Age, Enlisted

What I enjoy the most about showrunning is having a vision that you're able to follow. The writing is fantastic. I love running a room, being with a bunch of people who are incredibly talented and who are helping you think out your vision and then adding to your vision so it becomes everybody's vision, really. It's amazing. Where you think, "I've got a handle on this," and then people come up with these ideas that are so much better than yours and you go down their roads, normally you would think, "Oh, group think." As a former stand-up comic, I always had a nightmare vision of what it would be like to sit in a room with other people and write. Instead, if you're with the right people and you've got the good goal, it's the greatest thing in the world. It becomes this huge tree of creativity. I love seeing it all manifest itself. When you're on stage and you see something you wrote three months ago and they're doing it, it's an amazing feeling.

What Makes a Good Showrunner?

To paraphrase a popular film meme, one does not simply just become a showrunner. It's often a years-long process of first breaking into the television-writing industry as a writer's assistant and then working your way up the ladder of episodic television staff-writing positions. It's in those production trenches, such as writing, producing, post-production, and management, where a writer may evolve into an eventual showrunner.

EPISODIC TELEVISION WRITING LADDER

WRITERS ASSISTANT
STAFF WRITER
STORY EDITOR
EXECUTIVE STORY EDITOR
CO-PRODUCER
SUPERVISING PRODUCER
CO-EXEC PRODUCER
EXEC PRODUCER
SHOWRUNNER

Not every writer who ascends to the executive producer level wants to be a showrunner. The sacrifice and multi-tasking required from the individual, or showrunning partnership, is daunting enough to keep many writers satisfied with never committing to these all-encompassing responsibilities.

For those who do grab for the showrunner's brass ring, there are many rewards—financial, creative, and collaborative—that can come of it. But it's also a job where inexperience, ego, and poor management skills can be the downfall of many a great writer. Experiencing life under a bad showrunner, or watching a great writer wilt under the pressures exerted by the job, is unfortunately a common experience for scribes in writers' rooms, but it's where cautionary lessons are absorbed for future reference. For those who have executed the job, there are clear delineations for those who do the job well and those who do not.

ANDREW MARLOWE, Showrunner: Castle

When I was a kid, I watched *The Muppet Show* religiously. I loved it. I loved its tone. To see a character like Kermit running this three-ring circus, dealing with all the big egos, in a weird way gave me a sense of what the job was like. When you go to film school, you spend a lot of time working on storytelling and production, but not necessarily managing an organization of 300–350 people and making the trains run on time, overseeing a factory where you're delivering a show every eight days. It becomes a real challenge, so the people I ended up modeling myself on were James T. Kirk and Kermit the Frog—big influences (Laughs).

JAMES DUFF, Showrunner: The Closer, Major Crimes

I think the one attribute you must have to be a good showrunner is a creative vision. You can't invite a lot of people to help you put together a show if you haven't envisioned it properly, and then you have to be able to listen to people who are helping you put together your vision, and you have to understand that vision has to expand to include all the people playing on your team. You must have the vision first. You must have a really good creative vision, a really good creative idea, before starting out.

RONALD D. MOORE, Showrunner: Battlestar Galactica, Outlander

I feel like there's a lot of balls to keep in the air, and that I'm constantly trying to keep balls in the air. I don't feel like it pulls at me and drags me under. I kind of enjoy it, to be honest. I enjoy being the person with the answers. I enjoy people asking me questions, exchanges like: "What do you think this should be?" "Well, that's what I think it should be." "Should we go left or right?" "We're going left." I like being that person. I like being in control, that's probably the bottom line to it. I enjoy the physical production of it, I like the set, I like the crews, and dealing with the actors. I like the creative dialog about it. Even dealing with the budget and the production hassles don't get to me. I maintain a fairly calm show because I think part of my job is to have a calm show. I think that part of the job of a showrunner is to set the tone for what you're doing. If I'm upset, everyone's upset. If I'm panicked, everyone's going to be panicked. If I have a lot of anxiety, there's a lot of anxiety everywhere you turn. If I'm not, if I'm calmer, people calm down more. If you act confident, it goes out to the rest of the production. Many times I've been standing on a set where we had some crisis where we had to do this, and this, and this. I'll say, "We're not curing cancer here, guys, it's just a TV show, so don't go crazy. Don't kill yourselves to do this. It's just a TV show. Let's make it the best show we possibly can, let's do our very best effort, and really do something we're proud of. But, keep it in perspective."

JOSS WHEDON, Showrunner: Buffy the Vampire Slayer, Firefly, Dollhouse

I think there's two kinds of showrunners: there are hoarders and there are sharers. I've worked with both. Sharers want to include everybody in the process. Obviously, they want people to get better; it means less work for them, and it means that the show will be better. Hoarders need to do it all themselves. They need to put their name on every script. They need to, if possible, rewrite every script. I never rewrite anybody if they get it right. That's a contract that I have with the writers. If you come along and we work this out and you figure out the formula and you put it on the page, it's going to air. I don't think it helps building the growth of the show if you don't incorporate other people because it's the tonnage of the thing. Maybe if it was the BBC and I was doing six episodes a year, I could be that guy. It also seems like a lonely way to work. The writers of my shows and staffs, they're my families. You want them to grow. A lot of them are enormously talented, but you want them to be partners and not just scribes.

Not All Writers Are Good Showrunners

As with all things in life, just because a person is good at one thing doesn't mean their skill sets transfer to every task they perform. With showrunning, the ability to write doesn't mean that the ability to manage will be inherent as well. In fact, writers are known to be a rather singular species, spending long hours alone with scary amounts of caffeinated drinks, getting a computer-monitor tan.

"I think a lot of showrunners would rather be in their own room dealing with the story and dealing with the writers," former *House* writer Pam Davis explains. "But you have to answer all the questions or else everything grinds to a halt, so it's a really great balancing act of being a producer and a manager and being a great writer, so not a lot of people have everything it takes."

Which begs the question of what could possibly go wrong, assuming that every writer will be a gifted people person and decision maker?

A lot.

JEFF MELVOIN, Showrunner: Army Wives

The skill set to be a good writer and to be a good manager are, one could argue, almost diametrically opposite. I think writers tend to be skeptics and critics. They are fueled by anger, by curiosity, by outrage, and you've always got your nose up against the glass of whatever particular world you're trying to peer into. It's important to be wary and to be skeptical and to trust essentially nobody but yourself. A writer's stock in trade is your own sensibility and your own vision.

Whereas when you're managing writers, the idea is to be diplomatic, generous, to be a good manager of your own time, and to consider where other people are coming from. You have to be a psychologist in terms of you have so many aspects of production to be concerned about. The writers are your most immediate, but then you have to deal with actors, you have deal with the directors, and you have to deal with everybody else. You've got to manage upward to the studio as well as managing downward to all the people who report to you. Those skills are not innate, and when you spend a lot of time just trying to steer your own boat as a writer and develop confidence in your own vision and try to protect that, the idea now that you have to be doing all these other tasks can be overwhelming.

RONALD D. MOORE, SHOWRUNNER: BATTLESTAR GALACTICA, OUTLANDER

If there's a mistake I've made over the past few years, it's thinking that everyone can do this. Not everyone has those particular skill sets to run a show. What I take as sort of obvious—and it's not really rocket science to run a TV series—other people are quite challenged by it. I don't say that with ego. I think that certain people are adaptive to certain things, or have certain skill sets.

PAM DAVIS, PRODUCER: INTELLIGENCE

Qualities that a showrunner needs to do the job well: it's kind of a mixture of great writer and storyteller and great manager, which is really not a common combination. You need to be able to kind of see a big-picture story, and be able to give notes effectively so you can build the story and work with a writer well without just taking over, because the more work your writer does for you story-wise the less work you can do. You can take something great and make it even better or you can overstep and kind of end up working constantly.

The management part is really a tough thing for writers because we're generally sitting alone in a room somewhere, and then all of a sudden you get a show and you have to be in charge of 800 different departments and you have to prioritize what goes where, and you'd rather, probably, be sitting alone in your room dealing with a story. But you have to deal with a hundred people asking you a hundred questions, so it's a combination.

ROBERT KING, Showrunner: The Good Wife

It's a sticky question because if you're a creator of a show, that doesn't necessarily mean you have the muscles to run a show. Running a show is a technical operation, too, not just creative. Are you going to get the scripts in on time? Are you going to be able to supervise the directors correctly? Are you going to cast a show? Showrunners cast too; they're responsible for every element. The difficulty sometimes in doing that is that it's not attached to the personality and the confidence of the showrunner. We were very confident creators in that we knew exactly what the show was going to be. We knew where we wanted to head. We had very strong opinions about it.

ANDREW MARLOWE, Showrunner: Castle

It is an interesting transition to go from the guy who is the feature writer living in your own head to somebody who is now trying to articulate a vision to everybody else and also being a leader in the room, and that's not something that is necessarily taught. It's something that you have to feel your way through and learn. There are some people who are natural leaders and some people who are big personalities, but everybody has to find their own style. There are certainly tales of folks who don't do it well and have extraordinarily dysfunctional rooms, and yet the show has turned out pretty well, but I aspire to try and make the organization run as smoothly as possible. It was a new skill set to conquer. When you are used to having the solution in your head, when you are used to, from the feature universe, going off and thinking about it and then coming back with a solution, transitioning into making that process public and putting it up on the board, having everybody jump in, that was kind of new for me and that was a skill set that I had to acquire along the way.

JEFF MELVOIN

Nobody's born knowing how to run a show, particularly writers. There's two things: [a writer] could have the disposition to be a good leader, but no experience or no exposure to those tools that can help them, or they just might not have the personality for it at all. It's not surprising that the good writers often don't make the best showrunners because you are always a parent. You are a parent to the cast, and you are a parent to your writing staff. That's really the way the thing functions. If you've created the show, you're literally a parent. You've brought these characters into life. You're the one who's making the decisions. If you choose not to see yourself as a parent, that doesn't mean that you're not a parent. It means you're a dysfunctional parent and everything that happens on your show can be related to what happens in the dysfunctional family. People start trying to go around you. Nature abhors a vacuum, so people start trying to make decisions. If you're a bad parent, they'll say, "Mom said this and Dad said that," and they'll try to get you to make decisions based on their own particular perspective.

JANET TAMARO, Showrunner: Rizzoli and Isles

When you're a showrunner, you're still in the middle. You have bosses: the studio and the network apply pressure from above. The actors and actresses from both sides. The crew and the staff from below. You absolutely have far more freedom to make crucial creative decisions, and you are not attempting to mimic someone else's voice. You are the voice. But instead of being responsible for bits and pieces of one or two episodes, you are responsible for everything from prep to production to post. That's in addition to breaking and writing scripts and managing the studio and network notes. It's like having more homework than you can possibly do—with a final exam looming every time a script is due. Your job is actually multiple jobs that funnel into a single position. I was lucky. I'd had experience managing crews as a reporter. I'd also had a lot of production and post-production experience in that first news career. Most writers don't get those experiences. But that still isn't everything you need to know.

Once you create a show, you're suddenly tasked with running a complicated, collaborative business. A studio effectively hands you millions of dollars and says, "Go hire hundreds of strangers and make a bunch of movies with them."

Showrunning requires all kinds of skills that go well beyond writing. But if you want your vision realized, and you want a unified tone and look, you have to learn all these new skills—and learn them fast."

DEE JOHNSON, Showrunner: Boss, Nashville

It's so funny because on television everybody who is a showrunner pretty much is a writer, and that's almost always the way it's been except in the early days so it's difficult for me to separate the two. But I suppose that if you are unable to maybe standup for yourself and rewrite people, you kind of have to be able to do that and live with yourself. I suppose if you couldn't do that then it wouldn't be a good fit. I also think that for television it's so collaborative and, particularly in broadcast, you will be doing this huge number of episodes. You have to be able to work well with others.

SHAWN RYAN, Showrunner: The Shield, The Unit

You know, you have an army at your disposal when you're showrunning, and that army can be very effective if they have orders. Where I've gone awry is where I've let one area of what I'm doing fall behind and I have to turn all my attention there, and now, all of a sudden, you have this whole army over here that doesn't have orders and so they're sitting around and not doing the job they need to do. And therefore, when you finally finish and you come back you're like, "Whoa, why aren't we further along here?" Well, it's because I didn't give them direction along the way, so really it's a time-management issue. It's knowing that while I'm over here, the people over there have their orders and they're working.

KURT SUTTER, Showrunner: Sons of Anarchy

Shawn Ryan is a buddy of mine and I see him quite often, and [we] have these discussions sometimes. The interesting thing on *The Shield* is that Shawn was a baby writer when he was handed that show. He wasn't an established showrunner, and I think because of that he was very open in terms of process. Not that now, as a seasoned showrunner, he's not, but at the time it was all very new to him. I think it was the experience of having him as a mentor but also as a guy who was sort of in the process of discovering how to do it, as I was. I had never been staffed on a show before or written TV, other than specs. He was a guy with a couple of years of experience in TV who had never run a show before. I feel like we both went to school a little bit on the show. I think I learned my foundation for how I approach the world from Shawn in terms of how I run the room, and how I deal with my actors. Shawn is just a guy who was very aware of allowing writers to participate and have their own voice. He always had an open-door policy with the actors in terms of the script, not necessarily to allow actors to change the script, but at least you have the door open and say, "Come in and talk to me if you don't understand something."

SHAWN RYAN

I wouldn't be a showrunner if I hadn't written a script that somebody loved. You know, when people ask me what I do, I never say I'm a showrunner. I say I'm a writer—it's a very important distinction. I spend far more time showrunning than I do writing, and yet in my head and heart I'm a writer. Everything I'm doing is to support and defend and protect the writing and the stories that we're trying to tell. But if you can't sit down and crank out that script that makes the actors go, "Ooh, can't wait to play this," that makes a studio go, "Ooh, this is great," that makes the network go, "Ooh, this is going to be a great episode to have on the air," then you can be the greatest manager of people in the world, but what are you doing and what are you telling, you know?

The Co-Showrunning Paradigm

With the demands of the executive producer position requiring so much time and attention, many have chosen to embark upon the position with a creative partner. Many writing teams such as Robert and Michelle King (*The Good Wife*), Adam Horowitz and Edward Kitsis (*Once Upon a Time*), or Tara Butters and Michele Fazekas (*Agent Carter*), have used their long-term writing partnerships to their advantage, splitting showrunner tasks to make the position more manageable. If a co-showrunner dynamic is a choice from the start, it often creates some of the most stable behind-the-scenes environments, because there are two ears to bend in a day, and they work in tandem.

However, with the increased demand for scripted programming, there is a newer trend of original spec pilot ideas being bought from less experienced writers, or feature-film writers. Despite the idea's worthiness for greenlighting, that doesn't mean studios and networks are keen to hand over multimillion-dollar television budgets to creators unfamiliar with the intense demands of scripted production. And thus, there's been an uptick of concept creators being paired with veteran executive producers who know the rigors of achieving script and post-production deadlines.

In theory, it forges a creative partnership that allows the creator to feed and guide the ideas for a season's worth of scripts, while the day-to-day management of the show is also being fostered by a seasoned professional. In practice, it can be a forced partnership that's more about financial needs than creative synergy. In the best case scenarios, the creative team finds a middle ground and the pairing moves forward finding their own balance of duties. Or in some instances, the placed executive producer mentors the new creator enough to walk away by the end of a freshman season with the network and studio content that a stable foundation has been created and can be maintained.

Perspective is everything, and the following spectrum of writers and co-showrunners from married teams (the Kings) to separated partnerships (Jeff Pinkner and J.H. Wyman) are very frank about what works and what doesn't work about the dynamic.

Co-Showrunners From the Start

The easiest way to have creative people work together is when they choose to do it, and this variation on the co-showrunning model is obviously the smoothest because (at least initially) they want to steer the series ship as a partnership.

MICHELLE KING, Showrunner: The Good Wife

Frankly, I have absolutely no idea how single showrunners do it.

ROBERT KING, Showrunner: The Good Wife

I don't know either. The bottom line is that there's literally so much to do every step of the way. If we didn't have each other to do it, I think we would go crazy. I think there are showrunners who go crazy or go down into addiction. I think we keep each other from doing that, although sometimes I wonder about you. (*Laughs*)

MICHELLE KING

I think it's easier [being married as well]. The fact that our day together doesn't end makes it easier. The fact that we don't have resentful spouses at home makes it easier.

ROBERT KING

I think we kind of rely on each other a lot. It's not wrong to say we're happily married. That's a good place to start. Then there aren't all these little things that crop up that make you divisive, because you're dealing with them together.

JOHN ROGERS, Showrunner: Leverage, The Librarians

What are our duties on *Leverage* as showrunners? Drinking. Drinking is a big one. (*Laughs*) It's odd, because we aren't actually writing partners. We're actually friends who came up with the idea for the show at the same time Dean [Devlin] was developing it and we folded together. Chris [Downey] had been doing half-hours and I'd been doing features. We came in at this without any real example of showrunning, except comedy showrunning. We really came at it like a comedy room. We're all in a room together, we break the stories together. As far as the administrative stuff, I tend to follow a little more on that because I got a bit of a sense of it. When I'm doing that, he's driving the stories in the room. It's very flexible. It's whoever is in the room at the time. The writers are always on set when they're shooting. Sometimes I'll be on set. Sometimes he'll be on set. I was directing, so I was up for that. He took over the whole duties of the room during those weeks. It's pretty much who has got the free hand at that moment.

BEING PAIRED TOGETHER

This dynamic can get prickly when networks or studios decide to introduce creatives to one another and/or demand they co-showrun. Sometimes it's because the executive producer is under a development deal where a part of their contract is to jump into problem shows to help tinker, or get a show off the ground. As you can imagine, there's a lot of potential for egos to be bruised or feathers to be ruffled. "I have been in this chair before and it can be very fraught," showrunner Dee Johnson says candidly about her repeated stint coming onto shows such as *The Good Wife* and *Nashville* as a network mandated executive producer. "The arranged marriage of it can be really fraught. It becomes a bit of a dance and it has to find its footing. It's not an ideal scenario though most of the time. Rarely does it work out where everybody is loving each other."

But sometimes, the executive producers are open to the arranged marriage, like when J.H. Wyman was brought in to assist Jeff Pinkner co-showrunning *Fringe* in its second season, or feature writer Jonathan Nolan was paired with Greg Plageman after *Person of Interest*'s pick-up at CBS.

J.H. WYMAN, Showrunner: Fringe, Almost Human

What [Jeff Pinkner and I] do on *Fringe* is 50-50 everything because it's a difficult job. It's a big show. There's so much on the writing side. There's so much on the producing side. There's so much on the editing side. It's just great that we have each other to count on. If I'm doing writing, he's doing editing. It becomes easier to actually succeed because it's very tough in television; if you fall behind you're done. This allows us not to fall behind. We trust each other very much, so it's okay. I know that if he's looking after something that we're okay and, hopefully, he feels the same.

GREG PLAGEMAN, Showrunner: Person of Interest

I had worked with Warner Brothers on a couple of shows. I had met Jonathan [Nolan] through them when I was developing another project. We hit it off. We have some similarities in our background and, admittedly, it's not a genre that I had done before, but I took to pretty quickly. I think we get along pretty well.

I honestly think some of these shows, the scale of them on broadcast television, they're not really ideally suited to one person running them because there's so much work from the writing, to the room, to the casting, to editing. It's just constantly backing up. There'll be 22, 23, episodes a year, which is an older model, but it's a treadmill where if you fall, you hit your head, and you never get up.

JONATHAN NOLAN, Showrunner: Person of Interest

It's fucking bananas! We do panels with other showrunners, the cable guys, and they're always very nice to us, but they treat Greg and I like refugees from a leper colony. It's a little bit like, "How the fuck are you guys making this many episodes of TV, and trying to make them well? It's a crazy business model." It's one of the reasons why I wanted a partner on the show, and I was incredibly excited that Greg was willing to come on board, because I knew enough through my wife's [Lisa Joy, writer for *Pushing Daisies*] experience, to know that this is a crazy, crazy fucking job. It's a really cool one, but it is a crazy one. It doesn't make any sense.

It's like a controlled plane crash every week to get through that many scripts, and try to make them great.

So yes, there are occasions when we divide and conquer for the most part. We try and weigh in together on things, and often one of us will go in on post on a given episode, and we largely rotate on that, and someone else will try and keep the home fires burning. And then [for] production, we shoot everything in New York. We post and write out of this building [in Los Angeles], and we try and get one of us out to set at least once a month, just to make sure, but the show does run itself pretty well. You flatter yourself into thinking that you have to be there, or it'll fall apart. It's not going to fall apart. They run a great shop out in New York for us, but we do like to get out there as often as we can, just to make sure that it's one conversation, it's one show, and everyone is still working together.

ANDREW MARLOWE, Showrunner: Castle

It's fair to say that I was firmly ensconced in the feature universe and I hadn't come up through television. I'd written a couple of freelance episodes of some shows when I was first getting started but didn't really know about the machinery. I had friends in TV. We talked about the writers' room, but I was coming in from an outsider's point of view, so the first season they teamed me up with a guy (Barry Schindel) who was relatively seasoned. He was a great guy but ultimately I had pretty good clarity of vision of what I wanted, and by the third episode I was de facto running things, but absolutely with his help and with his support. One of the things I love in life is the steep learning curve. I found it exhilarating to get in and learn what everybody did and try to master enough of it to be able to know what everybody was talking about and be able to make decisions.

When Conflict Creates Disharmony

But what about when it isn't rainbows and puppies behind closed doors? Even when a collaboration is going right, there will be bad days of conflict. In a situation where there's an imbalance of power (especially when an executive producer has been appointed), can a partnership move forward, or does it create irreparable damage? A few showrunners explain the repercussions of disharmony.

JEFF MELVOIN, Showrunner: Army Wives

I had a tremendous disagreement with [the creator] about how the first season [of *Army Wives*] should end. It was a respectful disagreement. It was felt that for the end of the first season, she needed something really big, to really do a huge cliffhanger. What she had in mind was a soldier walking into a bar and blowing himself up and not letting the audience know who lived and who died. Personally, I thought that was against the spirit of what the show had done up to that point, and that it kind of jumped the shark. That was my thought.

Also, I was tired. I had been dropped into the middle of the situation [as a co-showrunner]. I didn't even have a chance to read the underlying book for weeks and weeks. I was on the show, breaking stories, and hadn't even had a chance to read the source material, that's how behind we were.

So I had very good talks with the studio and the network. I said, "Look, she's got this competing vision for this show. She created it. Let her do it." They said, "Well, we can't let her run the show because she doesn't have enough experience as a showrunner." I said, "That's fine, but I think we've come along far enough that it wouldn't be comfortable for us to continue to work together, just because I don't quite share what she wants to do with it." But we parted as friends, and remain friends, which is unusual. Part of what it was that it made easy for me to walk off was I was tired, and I felt I had done what I was asked to do, which was to put that show on its feet. I was very proud of it. I wished it well. [Melvoin returned to solely run the show from seasons 3-7.]

ALI LEROI, Showrunner: Everybody Hates Chris

Honestly, it was difficult [co-showrunning with Chris Rock]. It was very, very difficult. It changed Chris and me. It changed our relationship because you come into the show as creative partners, but there's a structure. The structure here is he's Chris Rock and I'm Chris Rock's guy. Then Chris Rock goes off and does something else and then I'm actually the guy left there to make decisions, so I *have* to make decisions. Creatively, what our relationship has been is that I'm almost functioning as a muse. I help him get his ideas out, but then if he leaves for two or three weeks, the show must go on, so now I got to make decisions.

But Chris is a very hands-on, creative person, so that was tricky because if I'm making certain decisions that he's not 100 percent on board with, or he's not 100 percent sure about, he's got to wait to see how it plays out. Suddenly he's in an incredibly uncomfortable position. He actually has to trust in a way that he's not accustomed to trusting. Even if he trusted me before, he was still in the next room. Now he's four states over and three weeks away and he hopes that whatever he sees—that he's going to be credited with or blamed for—meets his approval.

On the one hand it's tough because you have a creative relationship that you had established over a number of years. You have a friendship which you've established over a number of years, but the dynamic is changed. Really, in the truest sense of the word, I used to work *for* him. When we were doing HBO's *The Chris Rock Show*, I was there because Chris wanted me there, and we worked very closely in getting his ideas out, but he was the showrunner. He was actually making the decisions. Then when we go to a studio and a network, I'm actually the showrunner. I'm the guy that's there every day and I'm talking to the network. I'm talking to the studio executives. He's familiar with them but

I'm actually developing a relationship, and when they have a problem, they call me. Hopefully I can get him and get an answer. And if I can't get him and get an answer, based on whatever the practical aspects of what we're dealing with are, I've got to make a decision. I've got to hope that whatever decision I make, he's happy with it. In the plus percentile, he is, and every now and again he's not. Then we got to try to figure out how to hash that out, because he can't be sure. He's got to wait until it goes on. Now he just has to sit and wait until that decision appears on the air and he has to see whether he thinks it hurt him or whether he thinks it's helping him. Nobody can tell him how that feels. He has to make that decision himself.

It's any creative process. When you're really vested in it, all these little things make a difference. He actually was put, I think, in a very uncomfortable position. It was a position that he's absolutely 100 percent unaccustomed to being in. He was allowing his comedy vision to be managed by someone else. That someone was me. It's Chris Rock; he's one of the greatest comedians ever. It would literally be the same thing as him going, "Why don't you take my act and go say it. See what that looks like."

Losing a Co-Showrunner

In the case of *Fringe*, Jeff Pinkner bowed out of his executive-producer role just prior to the show's final season for many reasons including feature writing opportunities. It left J.H. Wyman as the sole showrunner for the last 13 hours of the series, a position he was completely comfortable assuming, yet admits was still a creative loss.

J.H. WYMAN, SHOWRUNNER: FRINGE

Running the show solo has its challenges on a whole bunch of levels. Number one, it's just so much fun to be a part of something with another person. You get a different perspective on things. But our group has been so involved in each other's lives and thinking. We've all influenced each other so well: J.J. [Abrams] and Jeff or Akiva [Goldsmith] and the writers that we use all the time. Now it becomes a lot more about my own personal view of things, how I like to tell stories, because one has to adjust. I don't want to say, "compromise," because compromise, for me, has a negative connotation, but I mean adjust. You'll say, "Well, I wouldn't handle an element that way, but I can see why that's important to you. I'll go with that and let's do that." That probably comes a lot from being a musician and being able to do my part and then everybody does their part. Then together, that's the sound. I quite enjoyed having Jeff and having that. It's really fun. That said, with the show coming into that last season, it was very clear where I personally wanted to go.

WHAT A NETWORK AND A STUDIO EXPECT FROM A SHOWRUNNER

When looking at the chain of command in television, the showrunner is responsible for overseeing the cast, producers, directors, and everyone in the crew (or those below the line). While it may seem like the pinnacle position, the showrunner is actually beholden to the network, which licenses and broadcasts their show, and the studio, who helps finance the production of the series. Those two entities represent the purse strings, and the bosses of a showrunner. The showrunner's function is not only creative, but also serves to ensure that the financial backer's investment has the potential to recoup their money and eventually become profitable when the series is eligible for syndication or foreign-market sales. Because of that, most showrunners understand that adopting a maverick attitude against their financial overlords isn't the smartest way of handling creative conflicts.

Instead, most showrunners have figured out their individual ways of making their bosses happy without selling out creatively to every whim of often jittery studio and network executives. It's a high-wire act that often needs a lot of adjustments as the seasons proceed, which these showrunners explain.

JOHN ROGERS, SHOWRUNNER: LEVERAGE, THE LIBRARIANS

We go to a bunch of people and ask them to give us a couple million bucks a week to tell our little pretend stories. The idea that they should do that with no strings attached is madness. It's other people's money. There are stockholders out there somewhere. I don't know who would invest in television now—that's a horrible idea—but in theory, that's other people's money we're playing with. We should involve them in the process and be open to the idea that you get some feedback. Don't try to drive us, but tell us what road you want us on, and we'll do the best we can.

CHRIS DOWNEY, Showrunner: Leverage

Ultimately, it's a business where there is a number. There's a number at which you survive and there's a number at which you don't survive. You get feedback; it's called ratings. Beyond what critics say about the show or what feedback you get on the websites, you look at the ratings and you see whether or not you're succeeding or failing. We respect that aspect of the business. We understand that the network has to maintain a certain number of eyeballs on their show or else you're gone.

HART HANSON, Showrunner: Bones, The Finder, Backstrom

The license fee is the amount of money that the network pays the studio for the show, and they get to broadcast it for that license fee. Then the studio turns around, and sells the show around the world and sells it into syndication to another network or cable. The studio has a whole bunch of ways of making money in secondary markets. [With *Bones*] Fox, the network, is the primary client. It behooves Fox, the network, to have the studio pay tons of money for the show, because it looks fantastic. It behooves 20th Century Fox TV to keep their budget down so that they're making as much profit as they can simply from the license fee so that all the other sales are gravy. Those are different agendas, and I have to contend with that. Every showrunner has to contend with the studio and the network. They very often fight through the show, not here. There is some cross-pollination with executives. The studio executive and the network executive can meet and have a coffee and hash things out, but it happens less than you would think.

SHAWN RYAN, Showrunner: The Shield, The Unit

As a showrunner, I always view things like a bank. You can deposit into a bank and you can withdraw from a bank. And at the beginning of my shows, I would always spend time depositing. Meaning, I would prove to the network that a) I knew what I was doing, then b), ask them to give me notes, but I'm going to react to them in smart ways, and if I disagree, I'm going to tell you why and you're going to be proud of the final product. Once you establish that relationship, you get an incredible amount of leeway.

You know, while I was doing *The Shield*, I also did *The Unit* for CBS with David Mamet. There wasn't a single story we wanted to do that we weren't allowed to do on that show, but it comes from building trust. You can withdraw things that you want so long as you made deposits along the way with these people. And so it really comes down to the fact that they have a lot of things to worry about at the studios and networks. Therefore, my plan is always to, as quickly as possible, become the least problematic show for them, because they only have so many hours in the day. And they're going to focus where they think their biggest problems are. So if my show is the least of their problems, then they're off giving notes and trying to save some other show, and that's when I'm allowed to do what I want.

DEAN DEVLIN, EXECUTIVE PRODUCER: LEVERAGE

In Hollywood, a lot of people get paid money to have opinions, and they feel that if they don't express that opinion they're not earning their money. So very often you have a lot of input that's not necessarily constructive. At TNT, the dialog is much more like two entities trying to do something together as opposed to "we're your boss and we want you to do this because our market research says so." They really approach it in a very old-fashioned way that I don't see even at the studios right now. Back in the day it used to be that a studio would gamble on a filmmaker and if the movie did well, they all felt great and got raises. If the movie tanked, they all got fired. Nowadays it's much more manipulated. It's more calculated. The experience of working with TNT has been like a throwback. They give us an enormous amount of freedom and when they have notes it's because they care deeply about something. And even then, you can have an adult conversation. It's such an unusual experience that I'm drawn back to it over and over again.

JOHN ROGERS

We don't ever tell people the scripts will be great. We assure them that they will like our work and we will work hard. It's interesting. [Chris and I] both worked for guys, and with guys, like this where they consider the sales job to continue past the pilot and all the way through the first season or even the second season, selling to the network again and again and again about how great the show is. I think we're both of the opinion that, "Here is the script, here's the work, here's the show. You like it, great. If you don't, then we should go work for people who like our stuff and you should just go find people whose stuff you like."

DAVID SHORE, Showrunner: House

You know what? I'd like to sit here and go, "Dammit, every time we try and do something different, [Fox] stands in our way and we run roughshod over them." They've actually been very good. Whenever we've done a departure episode, with a couple of exceptions, they've been extraordinarily supportive. They've welcomed it. Even in season one when we did the first departure episode, which was "Three Stories," they were excited about it right out of the gate, and we spent a little extra money on it.

HART HANSON

I'm not positive that the writers of shows should be the showrunners. I'm not 100 percent there. I'm glad it's worked out that way because it's been to my advantage, as I'm a writer. We can be very self-indulgent. I think writers can get a little bit precious about our work, and when we're the bosses, the only people who are going to draw that to our attention are probably the studio and the network executives. I'm not someone who would say I wish they didn't exist. It is born for friction, but I think we need them, and out of that friction comes better work.

Joss Whedon: The Unexpected Rebel

As the former executive producer of *Buffy the Vampire Slayer*, *Angel*, *Firefly*, *Dollhouse*, and now *Agents of S.H.I.E.L.D*, Joss Whedon has had more than his share of documented struggles with networks who didn't understand, or have the patience, to foster his particular brand of cult shows. More surprising to Whedon is the lore that's circulated about how he's pushed back on those executives. He sets the record straight on his "rebellious rep" and his actual view about his responsibility to the networks.

Joss Whedon

" I've probably spoken out against the behavior of the people at the top in the networks two or three times in my career. And now, I find recently that I have a reputation. The very first time I ever disagreed with one network head, he brought out the word difficult. 'Well, if you're gonna be difficult...' I'm like, 'Wow. I've pretty much given you everything you've asked for, for four years, actually five, and this is the first time we've ever disagreed,' and boom, here comes the rep. I have had mostly extremely good relationships, not just with network heads, but with standards and practices people; the kind of people, and younger executives, who are supposed to be the enemy. When you're doing a show, they can be the enemy, and sometimes they have been. They absolutely have. Obviously with *Firefly*, it was us against them and it was a sad state of affairs to be in. But that's not how I operate. I am, and always have tried to be, a company man.

I treat showrunning and this work of being in Hollywood like the Army. I take the orders that I'm given, even if I disagree with them, because one day I intend to be giving them and will expect the same.

That goes back to the first shows I worked on, the first movies. I don't step out of line. Sometimes I look back and go, 'Maybe I should have.' Part of me is just pathologically afraid of conflict, and part of me also just doesn't understand what kind of power I might have. In the instance of saying, 'Well, it wouldn't have mattered if I had fought for *Angel*,' it might well have mattered if I had fought for *Angel*, it just never occurred to me that you could.

That was after a time with having a great relationship with the WB and then having them kick *Buffy the Vampire Slayer* to the curb because they got into a shouting match with Fox. I think everybody's at fault there. Those business decisions can offend me, but they are not really part of my life. It's really the day-to-day workings of the show where I will do everything in my power to make the thing palatable to people who are putting up millions and millions of dollars to make the thing happen, and who have an absolute understanding of their network that I don't. They should have a say in what's going on.

Yes, I like to be left alone to do my thing. Everybody does. But the moment you forget that the executive you can't stand, who has never been helpful at all, might be the only person in the room who has the right idea about how to fix something, the moment you forget that, you're going to lose.

I know a lot of stories of great showrunners who are like,

'And I told the network, go fuck yourself, and I kicked them out and I shut the door.' I've never done that. I've gotten a little bit shirty and I've gotten insistent and I've drawn the line. I've put myself in a position to draw the line and I think that's an important part of it. I never needed to put a show on the air, so I never had to become so craven to the network that I hated them for it.

When I did *Buffy the Vampire Slayer*, I said, 'This is exactly the show we want to do. If you want a show that's sort of similar, then God-speed. I'm going to do something else with my life.' And therefore, because I had that absolute clarity, it was easy for me to be giving in other areas. I don't think you need to treat anybody like your enemy unless they are actively trying to destroy you, which occasionally does happen. There are those kinds of people out there, but there are not many. Everybody has a pretty good will and if you can tap into that and make allies out of everybody, things are going to just go much better. Yet now, I find that I'm this hot-headed maverick, which is amazing because I'm afraid of four-year olds. **"**

How the Showrunner Job Has Gotten More Complex

With increasingly fractured audience viewing patterns, technology moving faster than revenue models can keep up, and more and more competition over the digital-channel landscape, there's so much more than just writing great stories for a showrunner to think about now: quality scripts, social-media presence, ratings with DVR adjustments, and so on. Showrunners feel the constant pressure of being pulled in even more directions, and in ways no one could have anticipated even five years ago.

ANDREW MARLOWE, Showrunner: Castle

Television has become really compelling because it's in a fight for survival. Entertainment has become so diverse because you have the Internet, you have gaming. You have a hundred channels of niche entertainment for the folks who are interested in bass fishing or exploring the Amazon or finding crazy stuff at yard sales. It's fractured the audience in a way that we haven't really seen in our contemporary history. It's always kind of been the big three networks that have controlled everything, and before that a handful of radio stations, so the culture was all having the same conversation.

What's happening now is that we're going to this more specialized, niche programming which has forced conventional broadcast television to become much more competitive. It's forced it to become better just to survive. The level of storytelling is just much more sophisticated in your average show that takes place now versus your average show from 20, 30 years ago. There are a lot more moves because we're all trying to break through the noise. We're all trying to find an audience and make them think that our hour's worthwhile. I think those evolutionary pressures make the job difficult but also really exciting because you can't rest on your laurels these days. You always have to be pushing your storytelling into new territory. You can't just say, "Okay. I have an audience. I'm going to cruise for a season or two." You always have to be continuing to think how you are going to build that audience. How are you going to challenge the audience so they don't get bored? How are you going to do new storytelling? On *Castle*, every season we take a look at what we've done and we look at growing the characters or going into some sort of new paradigm that allows our characters to view the world in different ways than we've seen in previous episodes or previous seasons. I think it's really the responsibility of the showrunner to continue to figure out how to push stuff forward.

JEFF MELVOIN, Showrunner: Army Wives

With so many balls in the air, you'd think it's difficult sometimes to sort it all out, but I find that when you're actually in the middle of it, it can be very exhilarating. If you get fatigued everything becomes excruciating, but when I'm feeling energized it's a challenge and it's one of those things, like a guy spinning so many plates, where you actually feel kind of cocky about the whole thing. It's almost like playing 30-second chess and you're playing with six different people; move that, do this, do that, and you're walking into an editing bay and you're making a decision and you're coming back into the writers' room making this decision. You're looking at a problem that's coming from the set and you're making a decision. That's when it's at its best. When things aren't going well, when you're tired, when you're getting too much network or studio interference or problems from the set, it can feel like you've got a thousand people tap dancing on your skull. That's not fun.

JOSS WHEDON, Showrunner: Buffy the Vampire Slayer, Firefly, Dollhouse

When you create something, you have to have this little man in your head that says, "This is going to live for the ages." You're trying to speak universally. Some people aren't. Some people are doing something else. I am constantly begging for everybody in the world to love me every second when I'm working, and sadly also in my life. You kind of go in expecting that people will respond to it and that they'll stay with it. It doesn't leave me. It's incorporated in me. When people come up and it's fresh to them as they've just seen it, or they still love it, or whatever it is, there's an element of, "Well, yeah," which sounds like hubris, but is really just this little piece of hubris that you absolutely need to continue for all the times that people are going, "That's never going to work."

JAMES DUFF, Showrunner: The Closer, Major Crimes

I'll tell you a really fun story. The assistant director's office is just down the hall. It's about 20 yards away, and we have a pre-production meeting in there every episode. One episode we wound it up, and we had several lingering details that we had to figure out. I was walking from that door to my office and that walk took me 30 minutes, because everyone said, "I just need five minutes," "I just need five minutes," "I just need a minute."

At the very end of it, the guy who was doing props at the time, Frank Brighton, said, "Mr. Duff, I'm sorry to stop you, but I just need five minutes." I said, "Frank, one day I'm going to walk from that office to this office and no one is going to care what I have to say about anything, so stop me, please, and ask my opinion. I have an opportunity to give my opinion and people are listening."

I think that's how you have to look at it; you have to look at is as an opportunity. If you embrace the opportunity, and you embrace the people who are helping, you realize that opportunity, and you have a much better shot of getting it done right. You have elected to live in a stress-filled environment when you come on to do this kind of job.

I would also like to say that there are 250 other people who will be doing this job with me. That's one of the things that I'm principally grateful for, and I know in my heart and in my bones that I do not have my own television show. A lot of people who are doing my job don't understand that. They think they do. I don't. I do not have my own show. No one has their own TV show. It takes 250 to 300 people giving it everything they've got every day of the week to have a good show. Mostly, though, I'm doing what the day brings me. I admit very much to being run by the show more than running the show myself. The show takes you and runs with it. You don't get to decide where you're going to go. The show decides where you're going to go, and the show decides when you have time to consider something else, anything else.

IN DEPTH:

WGA SHOWRUNNERS TRAINING PROGRAM

Jeff Melvoin is spot on when he says, "No one is born knowing how to run a show," but that doesn't mean you can't get officially trained to do the job well. Through the Writers' Guild of America, Melvoin helped create the curriculum for the Showrunners Training Program (launched in 2005) that was "designed to help senior-level writer-producers hone the skills necessary to become successful showrunners in today's television landscape." [1]

Jeff Melvoin explains that for those that want to create their own series concepts with the intention of executive producing the show into existence, the program empowers writers with real-life exposure to the day-to-day of showrunning.

WHY FORMALIZE A PROGRAM WHEN WRITERS CAN JUST LEARN ON THE JOB?

The impulse for the Showrunners Training Program came from a couple of directions. First of all, a friend of mine, John Wirth (*Terminator: Sarah Connor Chronicles*), another showrunner, worked together with me on the show *Remington Steele*. He had an idea to put together a book about the various jobs of what goes into being a writer and writer/producer in episodic television.

[1] **http://www.wga.org**, Showrunner Training Program.

There were about ten of us who started to assemble that. We thought it would take a year. It took us five years. John and I ended up editing it. It's a nice little volume and it's put out [free] by the Writers' Guild.

That kind of put the idea in my head about doing something on a different scale, on a different platform. One of the things that interested me was continuing education. The Guild does a great job of protecting writers in terms of contracts, pensions, and medical benefits, but I thought it had not done such a good job of capturing any collective wisdom or institutional memory about what it was to run a television show. In the old days, I don't think it was as necessary because there were fewer networks, fewer competition. The audience, frankly, wasn't as demanding.

WAS "SHOWRUNNER" ALWAYS A POSITION?

The way the business ran was that you had to be in the business for six to eight years before they would let you pitch a show, because the assumption was that if you pitched the show you would run the show. After six or eight years, the networks and studios had leached just about enough creativity from you that you were going to suggest something different, but not too different; fresh, but not too fresh, which is what they wanted. "My detective has a limp. My detective has a father-and-daughter combination. My detective is blind." Whatever it is, it was all variations on a theme and you could apply that to any of the genres.

I think that MTM Enterprises was largely responsible for the rise of the showrunner as an individual. The term wasn't in use until the late '80s or early '90s. In fact, the job wasn't there. Back in the '60s, when they did 39 shows in the season—as opposed to 22, which is a prime-time season today—there was essentially a non-writing producer, like a Sheldon Leonard (*The Andy Griffith Show*) or a Danny Thomas (*The Dick Van Dyke Show*), or a Quinn Martin (*The Fugitive*). There was a story editor and there was a freelance market. They did 39 shows that way and it worked.

What happened with the rise of MTM was that Grant Tinker recognized that if you put more responsibility in the hands of the writers, gave them more authority and gave them more back end, good things would happen. Plus you didn't have to pay them as much up front. With the rise of the comedies at MTM, *The Mary Tyler Moore Show*, *The Bob Newhart Show*, and then with the dramas, beginning with things like *The White Shadow*, *St. Elsewhere*, and *Hill Street Blues*, when those things caught on the studios were quick to follow. Suddenly the writer/producer became a much more important figure.

Then over the last 20 years, with the proliferation of outlets, cable in particular, not only was there a need for more shows, but also there was a need for more creativity. The idea of simply getting someone to say, "My detective is a father and son," that wasn't enough. There had to be fresher stuff coming in, which I think is a good thing, and so they began to look for writers who were younger, writers who had newer ideas, but writers who didn't necessarily have six to eight to ten years in television. This all coincided, so there's more slots being opened and there's younger and less experienced people. They don't necessarily have to be younger; there are a number of people that had considerable experience in film that started to come over to TV, but they had zero TV experience.

Another ramification of what was happening with the business is that shows were getting the hook earlier. The idea that you could get a show and the show was okay but it could run for five or six years—those were becoming rare. There's no better way to learn this business than to be on a show for two or three years. You can really see how things work, and learn. But if you're changing jobs every year or so, it's not conducive to really learning that much. That's especially so because in the life history of a show, the first six to 13 episodes are always frenetic. Changes are being made. You're being second-guessed left and right, and you can't really get into that kind of rhythm that I consider reasonable, and balanced habits and protocol can't be put into place where you can really produce the show professionally and get the best results out of everybody. You've got to throw your mother under the bus, if you need to, in those first six episodes just to keep it on the air.

You put all those things together and what happened, I think, as we came into the late '90s and the turn of the century, is that many more people were getting the job of creating a show or running a show with less and less experience and less opportunity to get that experience, because the apprenticeships were becoming fewer and farther between. That's what led me to think people could really benefit from having some sort of program in which they could, at least, be exposed to different ways that people do it.

What does a writer experience in the program?

The first week, it's going from writer to manager: what does it mean, what's the job, what's the history of it? Then, the second week is managing writers and the writing process. Then it's managing directors and actors, managing executive relationships, managing production, managing post-production, and then managing your career. By the time we're through, we've had directors come and talk to us about the job from their perspective. We've had actors talk about the job from their perspective. We've had unit production managers and location managers talking about their job. We've gone to a post house and had editors and cameramen talk to us about what the job is.

The idea is to give the class exposure to all the different tasks that go into being a showrunner, but also to understand what other people's jobs are and what they look to you as a showrunner to do for them so that you can enable them to actually do their jobs.

What's a key lesson you want the writers to walk away from the program learning?

I reduce showrunning to: if you have to remember only one thing from the entire six weeks, it's four words: "quality scripts, on time." If you don't have quality scripts then what's the point of doing any of this? If quality scripts don't come on time you're going to be off the air. You're not going to have a quality hour because they couldn't do a quality hour because your script was late.

Is a goal to teach writers how to have a hit series?

No, most shows aren't smash hits. Most shows are living on that bubble and, at the end of the day when the network and the studio look at the hot costs and look at what the show has done, they say, either we want to be in business with that person again or we don't. How you acquit yourself is often as important, or more important, than how your first or second show actually performs, because if you stay in the race long enough, you're going to win. It's just a question of how you can stay in the race. Nothing will get you out of it quicker than arrogance, ignorance, and being over budget and behind schedule.

DO PARTICIPANTS FIND THEMSELVES MORE MARKETABLE AFTER TAKING THE PROGRAM?

I don't know if by going through the program, we can quantifiably say that it increases somebody's marketability. Anecdotally, we are hearing that that's increasingly true, that the program has a certain status, and that it is a relief, or a comfort or reassurance, for a studio and a network to know that someone has been through it.

JANET TAMARO, STP GRADUATE

" The Showrunners Training Program at the WGA was pretty great because so many showrunners shared their experiences. However, nothing prepares you for the near-incinerating temperatures of that actual showrunner's hot seat. I saved my notes, and when it got tough during my first season at the helm, I'd re-read them to remind myself that this is the gig: solving the problems.

"The Writers' Guild asked me to come and speak to a new group of potential showrunners. It was an out-of-body experience to be a panelist two years after I'd been a 'student.' I remember looking at that sea of hopeful faces and thinking, 'Damn. We were just as hopeful. And just as clueless.' "

CAN ANYONE GET INTO THE PROGRAM?

The program is very selective. You have to be either a writer/producer or you have to have development that's current. You have to be recommended by either a showrunner, or a network, or studio executive. We usually get about 90 applicants for 20 slots. We give out about 25 slots, but technically it's supposed to be 20. Out of those 90 applicants, we interview 40 and then we select about 20 or 25. That's the hardest part of the program. I hate having to eliminate anybody, but it makes the class much more interactive. Part of the value of the program is hearing from everybody else's experience, because that is part of the reason for the program: to share experiences and so people can learn from each other.

CHAPTER TWO

WRITING IS THE HEART OF A TV SHOW

THE SCRIPT IS KING

Now that we know what a showrunner is, the next thing to understand is the particular landscape in which they operate. The American television creative epicenter is still Los Angeles, California. While television series production has expanded far outside of southern California, with a large number of shows being filmed in New York City, Georgia, Louisiana, and Canada, amongst others,[1] the majority of television series writers' rooms are still located in L.A. regardless of its shooting location. So that means the big, creative brain trust for scripted television is still very centralized. It also has its own unique, creative season/cycle and structure.

Unlike the film world (which television shows co-exist with on studio complexes and in office parks), the contemporary television landscape is built around the writer. No, that doesn't mean studio and network executives throw flower petals in front of them as they enter their writing offices. It means in practice, the film world considers the director the ultimate voice of a cinematic vision. In television, the creators and showrunners who write the episodes and guide a show's season are the ones who maintain the creative reins. Is it any wonder film screenwriters have been flocking to television in the last decade as a place where their creative vision can finally stay within their purview?

[1] http://www.filmla.com/uploads/2013-Television-Pilot-Production-Report_1372185855.pdf

PILOT SEASON 101

For decades, the television industry has kept its world spinning by maintaining a consistent, annual system of creative renewal called "pilot season," where writers and concept creators pitch their ideas to studios and networks, that will in turn (hopefully) accept (or "greenlight"), produce, and schedule it as a new television show for audiences to consume.

Up until the explosion of scripted programming by basic cable channels and the new business model of creating viable and robust summer and winter seasons of television took hold at the start of the new millennium, the annual pilot season in Hollywood used to operate on a two-year cycle.

The typical process for broadcast television development would go as follows: studios accept new TV show pitches in the summer (July/August). Interesting or fostered ideas would then be developed into scripts during the Fall, for a possible greenlight in January to actually cast and produce that first—or pilot—script into an episode. Produced pilots would then be reviewed in late April by networks for a possible order to season by their original programming departments. In mid-May, the picked-up shows would be presented in New York City by the networks to potential advertisers at "upfronts", an industry event which basically funds the new and existing shows with advertiser commitments. Those selected few would then get to hire writing staffs, production teams, and cast by late May. Writing staffs go to work in June, with the start of actual production happening in mid to late summer. The debut of the series would then happen anytime from September to November.

JUNE

		1	2	3	4	5
6	7	8	9	10	11	12
13	14	15	16	17	18	19
20	21	22	23	24	25	26
27	28	29	30			

Studio accept pitches

JULY

			1	2	3
4	5	6	7	8	9	10
11	12	13	14	15	16	17
18	19	20	21	22	23	24
25	26	27	28	29	30	31

AUGUST

1	2	3	4	5	6	7
8	9	10	11	12	13	14
15	16	17	18	19	20	21
22	23	24	25	26	27	28
29	30	31				

SEPTEMBER

		1	2	3	4
5	6	7	8	9	10	11
12	13	14	15	16	17	18
19	20	21	22	23	24	25
26	27	28	29	30		

Pilots are written for accepted pitches

OCTOBER

				1	2
3	4	5	6	7	8	9
10	11	12	13	14	15	16
17	18	19	20	21	22	23
24	25	26	27	28	29	30
31						

NOVEMBER

	1	2	3	4	5	6
7	8	9	10	11	12	13
14	15	16	17	18	19	20
21	22	23	24	25	26	27
28	29	30				

DECEMBER

	1	2	3	4
5	6	7	8	9	10	11
12	13	14	15	16	17	18
19	20	21	22	23	24	25
26	27	28	29	30	31	

Network return notes for pilot first drafts

JANUARY

1	2	3	4	5	6
7	8	9	10	11	12	13
14	15	16	17	18	19	20
21	22	23	24	25	26	27
28	29	30	31			

Networks greenlight pilot scripts for production

FEBRUARY

				1	2	3
4	5	6	7	8	9	10
11	12	13	14	15	16	17
18	19	20	21	22	23	24
25	26	27	28			

MARCH

		1	2	3
4	5	6	7	8	9	10
11	12	13	14	15	16	17
18	19	20	21	22	23	24
25	26	27	28	29	30	31

Pilots begin filming

APRIL

1	2	3	4	5	6	7
8	9	10	11	12	13	14
15	16	17	18	19	20	21
22	23	24	25	26	27	28
29	30					

Networks decide on series pick-ups

MAY

| | | | | | | |

Series are presented to advertisers at upfronts in New York City

That was how it was done for a long time, and some networks still adhere to this cycle, like NBC and CBS. But basic cable, premium cable (HBO, Showtime, etc.), and streaming providers (Netflix, Amazon, etc.) have pulled away from that model and are now constantly developing new shows, because as appointment viewing (or watching TV at the scheduled time a show is aired) has all but disappeared owing to new technology options, so too has the usefulness of the traditional cycle. Even broadcast networks like Fox[2], as of 2014, may formally reject the costly and limiting system in favor of more rolling development and non-traditional series pick-up options (i.e. short seasons, event series, etc.).

"From the outside, it seems crazy," *The Shield* showrunner Shawn Ryan observes. "From the inside, it seems crazier, and yet there is something that works about it. There's a crucible that you get put through that sometimes allows things to happen. Hollywood is a town that works on deadlines, and this is the ultimate deadline. You're picked up in January. You've got to turn your pilot in by May 1st, and come May 15th you'll know. It is crazy that so many pilots should be made at the same time, and that resources are being divided up in that way, and yet somehow, you know there's one or two pilots every year that come out where people go, wow, that's kind of great."

And that's another reason the traditional pilot season cycle is also losing favor, because it encourages a costly system of wasteful spending and creative time. Of perhaps 100 developed shows (comedies and dramas), only a tiny percentage of pilots—in which millions have been spent to produce each of them into a final, viewable product—are actually ordered to air. It's the speed dating of creativity wherein the ideas and concepts that could use more time to be a solid series instead get rushed through the pilot-production phase and sometimes turned into a series when the idea isn't fully baked. However, the newer development models allow season arcs to be written, and sometimes full seasons to be written, before production happens, ensuring stronger freshman seasons, a better chance for a show to survive with demanding

[2] http://www.deadline.com/2014/01/tca-foxs-kevin-reilly-declares-network-is-abandoning-pilot-season/

audiences, and a sounder financial investment.

Creators/showrunners all admit feeling the heat during that traditional pick-up window in May.

MIKE ROYCE, Showrunner: Men of a Certain Age, Enlisted

"Rumor week." This is the week where everyone's handed in their screening. The networks are all screening what they have. They haven't made their decisions yet. You don't know what the hell's going on. You're just sitting there for about a week to ten days where you can't do anything. If you're smart, you're writing, which means I'm not that smart. No, I am actually working pretty hard. You're meeting writers and going, "If you *could* work on my show, it would be great." The next day it could be, "I have no show, it was nice to meet you." That's mostly what happens, because they pick up far fewer pilots than are actually made. You're odds are always terrible, always, no matter how great your pilot is. What should happen actually is when a show doesn't get picked up, you should all disappear into a mist because this is all just this mirage.

SHAWN RYAN, Showrunner: The Shield, The Unit

Each project's different. I think everyone, in their heart, knows the quality of what they're working on. You know you have to keep a little bit of your heart protected because it so easily couldn't happen. You don't know why [the networks] make the decisions they make in their cozy little rooms. There are terms that are important to them, like branding, that as a writer don't enter your lexicon very often. You work really hard to make this thing and you begin to care very, very much about it. And then people that you don't really know that well hold your little creature's fate in their hands, and when they crush it, it's hard.

I certainly think the other pilots are the competition. It drives you crazy a little bit to know too much about them. I remember when I made *The Shield* they were only making one other pilot, and I knew that one of the two would go. I got very worked up about this other thing, but refused to read it. I had the opportunity to see it at one point. I didn't want to see it. I didn't want to know anything about *that* pilot, or the people that made it, because I wanted to kind of secretly hate it. I didn't want to watch it and go, "Oh, well, that's actually kind of good." (*Laughs*)

Basic TV Act Structure

A s watching television has become more and more dominant as a cultural pastime, mainstream audiences have not only paid more attention to those who write it, but also the structure in which episodes are written. Granted, we know it's mostly critics, fledgling TV writers, and/or hardcore TV obsessives that pay attention to the structure in which a script unfolds, but that doesn't mean it isn't interesting, or have an incredible influence on the creative direction of a show.

To provide a little screenwriting 101, in the film world the three-act structure is the template that dominates screenplay writing. It's based on the Greek philosopher Aristotle's dramatic theory, *The Poetics,* from way back in 335 BC, which essentially explained that every good story needs a beginning, a middle, and an end.

Fast-forward to the television age where writers basically adapted one-act plays and three-act plays to the new medium. However, that traditional structure soon had to make space for advertising breaks, which essentially paid for the programme airing. Making a television show isn't cheap, and it's only gotten costlier. Thus, the three-act structure has expanded over the last 50 years to include an increase of commercial breaks (up to six in some hour-long shows) in both comedy and drama scripts, even though the allocated screen time has not changed (either 60 minutes or 30 minutes).

It's only in premium or streaming-based television shows—like *Boardwalk Empire, Spartacus,* or *House of Cards,* which aren't funded by advertising money but rather by subscriber fees—that showrunners still craft episodic stories in the three-act structure. There are no commercials, which means no ad breaks. But broadcast and basic cable television shows have to follow an act structure dictated by the network on which they air.

What does all of this mean? Essentially, that the majority of television writers have a fairly rigid template they have to write around. And it's not an easy task. Showrunners help build a pace and tonal structure for their shows around their network-mandated act breaks, while also using all of those moments right before commercial breaks (or act outs) as an opportunity to leave the audience surprised or compelled enough to stick around during the ads. It doesn't matter that so many of us fast-forward through our DVR'd recordings of a series, or binge watch on a streaming service where ads are moot. For now, the majority of the television industry still bases everything—even the creative flow of an episode—around advertising breaks.

JEFF MELVOIN, Showrunner: Army Wives

When you have to write for act breaks on broadcast television that means that you have to create space for commercials. You write your first act, which can be 10–12 minutes, and then you've got to break because they're going to put in three or four minutes of commercials. After that, you come back. Writing for act breaks becomes an art in itself, because you can work them to your advantage. They give you certain freedom to do things in terms of continuity, jumping ahead in the story, or creating suspense. They're not all bad, especially if you can zip through the commercials.

It's a very different concept than running an HBO show, for example, where there are no act breaks because there are no commercials. Also, they don't have to reach any specific length. We always, whether it's in cable, basic cable, or in broadcast, have a very strict amount of technical specs you have to meet every week. The story content [for a drama] right now on broadcast and basic cable is 42 minutes including a 30 second recap. Every show has slight variations, but it's always going to be [similar]. You can get variances, but the variances don't extend more than usual. You can never be over because that means that they would sell less advertising. You can never do that, but you can be under sometimes because then they can sell more advertising. But you don't want to be too far under every week, or they begin to not like that very much either.

JANE ESPENSON, Showrunner: Caprica, Husbands

When I came up in TV, dramas were in four acts. *Buffy The Vampire Slayer* was four acts and that means there were three commercial breaks. Let's picture a loaf of bread: the three cuts make four pieces of bread, and so you got used to structuring a story like that. There'll be a big turning point right in the middle of the loaf that changes everything, so it's not even going to be pumpernickel anymore when you come back to this loaf. Then it started changing, and we got to five acts, and then six acts, and now some shows are six acts and a teaser, or seven acts and a teaser. There's this inflation because they want to put more commercial breaks in, so you end up having to turn your story more often. You [write] six pages and you stop for a commercial break. Now you need that next six-page chunk when you come back to feel a little different in flavor than the first six pages, or that act break will feel like it didn't quite land. You end up having to make all these little turns in the story. The problem is you end up with a very shallow, twisty story.

ROBERT KING, Showrunner: The Good Wife

The six-act structure will destroy storytelling, only because, even though the network or the studio will say, "Oh, don't worry about having a strong act-out," when they come down to it, they want a strong act-out, which usually means throwing some bullshit nonsense explosion in there of some kind. We are in a better position, in that [*The Good Wife*] has a five-act structure. They call it a teaser and four, but our teasers are very long, like 12 minutes long, so they're really full acts. The problem is that you have to create strong act-outs that will pull people back, so it's not very friendly to storytelling; it's friendly to more "Bruckheimeresque" explosion storytelling.

MICHELLE KING, Showrunner: The Good Wife

We also have made a conscious decision to try to vary the structure from episode to episode which, hopefully, makes it a better viewing experience. It also makes it a more difficult writing experience for the writers in the room, and makes it more difficult to structure. We are trying to reinvent it all the time.

COMEDY VS. DRAMAS AND SERIALIZED VS. PROCEDURAL

Creatively, pigeon-holing is a fact of life in television writing. Once you fly your creative flag in a specific genre, there's a good chance that's all anyone will think you can write.

Is that true? Of course not, but the industry tends to use the last successful thing someone worked on as the template for an entire career. That's why there are such entrenched opinions amongst writers about the slipstream of television writing one may choose to embark upon.

For example, there's the age-old question of what's more challenging to write: comedies or dramas? The question isn't what's better (which is completely subjective) but does writing for one genre or the other make you a better writer, or train you to tell stories better?

Showrunners Andrew Marlowe, Mike Royce, and Bill Prady often weave both elements into their scripts and shows with equal finesse, and they ably make strong arguments for the challenges of both styles.

ANDREW MARLOWE, SHOWRUNNER: CASTLE

People always talk about what's harder to write: comedy or drama? I have a personal philosophy that what is hardest in writing is whatever you are doing at the moment. Whether it is breaking the story, whether it is coming up with a title, whether it is coming up with a joke or an interesting twist, what is most difficult is what you are doing at *that* time.

I think drama and comedy each present different kinds of challenges, and I also think that some are better suited to some writers than others. There are folks who are very quick-witted. They are very fast in the room and to them comedy is easy. Then there are other people for whom it is just banging their head against the wall trying to find that elegant joke. I think some of that's in the DNA and some of that's in the training. Then there are some comedy writers who come to drama and aren't used to the structure. They aren't looking at it from the point of view of how can a line service a multitude of aspirations where you are looking to reveal character, you are looking to move the story forward, you are looking to create conflict *and* it needs to be funny.

MIKE ROYCE, Showrunner: Men of a Certain Age, Enlisted

I think that comedy is harder than drama. I'll just say it. I just mean good comedy. Comedy where you're telling a story while making people laugh is doing two things at once. It's a hard thing. It's also much harder to perform comedy. It's especially hard when you see the best comedy shows, or I should say at least the ones I love the most like *Modern Family*. You see people in real situations and they feel like you know them yet you're laughing your ass off. That's an incredible thing. Those two things are so hard to balance. Most comedies don't feel realistic and you're not really buying what the characters are doing, or they don't make you laugh. To be able to do both those things at the same time, that's why there's not very many hit comedies.

BILL PRADY, Showrunner: The Big Bang Theory

The trick to writing comedy is the willingness to say the 99 stupid things that precede the one funny thing. I joke about that but there's a sort of natural, societal fear of embarrassment. When you're in a social situation, if something really funny occurs to you, you say it. There isn't a willingness to say, "I'm going to say 25 things until I get to the thing that makes you laugh." That's what happens in a writers' room. There's an unspoken, or sometimes spoken, agreement that we're just going to ignore the really, really bad joke pitches, and keep going until we find the funny one. The trick isn't being funny. The trick is a greater willingness to be stupid.

ANDREW MARLOWE

In dramas, characters, in my opinion, ought to change. In sitcoms not necessarily so much, because you're dealing with archetypes and people like to see how this particular character is going to respond to that particular situation in this way. In those situations, it's really up to those showrunners and that writing staff to come up with new and interesting ways to challenge those characters. I still marvel at *The Simpsons*. Five hundred episodes [and counting] and they're still figuring out new stuff to do without cannibalizing themselves.

BILL PRADY

A situation comedy draws its humor from the situation the characters are in, from the conflict between the characters. If you get to a place where you're stuck, and there's nothing funny that's happening here, the answer is usually in the structure of the scene, or in the structure of the episode. For example, if there's no conflict, there's nothing funny. If you don't have a character in opposition to another character, a character in opposition to himself and his own desires or to the situation around him, there's nothing funny about it.

At the same time, for some reason, you get into situations where it ought to be funny, and you'll get a spot that just refuses to be. There's a great nickname for this. Apparently years and years ago—and a lot of the slang goes back 20 or 30 years—Sonny Bono, the singer and, oddly, later politician, opened a restaurant in Los Angeles that failed. A series of restaurants went into the same spot and failed, one after another after another. Sometimes a spot in a script that refuses to hold a functional joke is a "Bono's."

ANDREW MARLOWE

In sitcoms you can get away with a premise for 22 minutes, and exploring that premise from a bunch of different points of view. You can't quite do that in an hour, so both of them I think are very different skill sets. It is kind of like asking what is harder to play: football or basketball? They each have their own challenge. They each have their own set of skills and muscles that you need to develop.

COMEDY WRITING WITH BILL PRADY

Bill Prady started his comedy writing career with *The Muppets*, so the man certainly has cred outside of co-creating one of the most successful sitcoms of the new Golden Age of Television: *The Big Bang Theory*. He'll often share comedy writing terms and concept explanations via his Twitter account, but shares a few more-complicated ones here.

" **A comic engine**: It could be anything that gives the scene a comedic urgency. It could be literal urgency, like a deadline, so speed is a comic engine of a scene. [In the classic *I Love Lucy* episode where they work at a chocolate factory], the literal speed of the conveyor belt is the comic engine of the scene. It could be embarrassment. It could be shyness.

Most comedy-show writers have a word that they'll use to describe that sort of indefinable quality that is the thing in the episode that tickles [interest] in that episode. David Crane, a great sitcom writer who co-created *Friends*, used a made-up word—'shtummy.' It's the thing in this episode that makes it authentic. You start with that for the episode then break it down to a scene in the episode and then you ask, within this scene, what's the comic engine of this scene?

The Donkey Problem: Let's say you write a very high-concept episode and you've got this great block comedy in the scene that has to do with somebody having a donkey and taking the donkey into their house and the donkey wreaking havoc on the house. But the scene in act one where they buy the donkey fundamentally makes no sense. You can't fix it. You bought the

> donkey. We try not to buy the donkey. We try not to lock into a high-concept ending, a big thing, or a sequence of episodes that lock us into bad story-telling on the way there. "

Another ongoing debate amongst one-hour television writers (and the industry overall) is what kind of episodic structure is more valued by networks and audiences. Serialized shows are ones where story arcs play out over many episodes, or seasons, like *Lost*, *Battlestar Galactica*, or *Game of Thrones*. Investment in every episode is requested of the audience, and in turn hopefully pays off with deeper characterizations, mythology, and complicated storytelling. On the other end of the spectrum are procedural shows where there's a case of the week that gets resolved in a contained, single episode, such as happens on *Law & Order*, *NCIS*, or *CSI*.

Networks typically have preferred procedural shows because audiences can jump in and out of watching episodes without missing important content or feeling left out of the mythology. The format isn't distancing for potential viewers and ratings. However, most showrunners and writers usually prefer investment storytelling in the serialized vein, and have even bridged the gap by creating the hybrid model which marries the case of the week resolution style of storytelling with the serialized stories, usually involving the character's personal lives over time. Is one truly better than the other? It depends on the showrunner you ask.

JAMES DUFF, Showrunner: The Closer, Major Crimes

The idea for [*The Closer*] to be a procedural actually came from the network. They gave me the genre and asked me to work within it. That was a very exciting experience for me because I had always wanted to write mysteries. I was much better known, if I was known at all, for writing family drama. It's my opinion that if you concentrate hard enough on family drama, you will eventually get to murder, and I was fortunate in that they let me do that.

The Closer is serialized in its characters a little bit, but you can skip five episodes of it and turn it on and catch right up. It's not like you're missing big beats, because we keep them all alive. Characters are serialized, and they're not static as most television characters are. We wanted that for a reason. We wanted the characters to slowly grow, so we sort of nourished that aspect of them.

CHRIS DOWNEY, SHOWRUNNER: LEVERAGE

I'll talk with some of my friends who write on traditional procedurals, and the hardest thing on those shows is the clue path. What's the clue path this week? Once they have an arena where they're going to be—like it's a murder in a circus, it's a murder at a microchip plant—they're in heaven. But finding a new clue path that they haven't done before, that's what they spend the bulk of their time on. For us, the clue path is the heist and the cons.

ANDREW MARLOWE, SHOWRUNNER: CASTLE

One of the things I've noticed on a typical procedural drama, which isn't character oriented, is that it seems like every season they have to find bigger and more sensationalistic storytelling to keep the audience engaged. I think you can be very successful at that for a while, but it becomes its own trap and it can't sustain itself. [On *Castle*] we're always looking at how we're continuing to engage the audience and how we're hoping to reengage them and reinvigorate the storytelling as we move forward. I think in a procedural especially, it becomes harder every season to find cases that are going to be engaging for your characters where you're not revisiting territory that you've been over before.

JANE ESPENSON, SHOWRUNNER: CAPRICA, HUSBANDS

I think it used to be the case that serialized stories were more the province of cable, and network preferred stand-alone. However, *Lost* was network. I think more and more serialized stuff has invaded all of it because of DVDs and DVRs. People no longer have to watch their show once a week, and therefore might find it hard to keep a complicated storyline in their head. More people will see your show on DVD than will see it when it's broadcast live that night.

You've got to keep in mind that most people are going to put in a disc and then put in the next disc and they're going to see it in a row. You can tell a complicated, very serialized story whether you are cable or broadcast. I think serialization just started at cable, but it's spread over the whole medium. I think that serialization is here to stay. It's part of what makes a powerful story.

RONALD D. MOORE, Showrunner: Battlestar Galactica, Outlander

The reaction to serialized storytelling at the networks is that they're very schizophrenic about it. They're afraid of it, and they love it. The thing everyone's most interested in at the studio and the network level is the longer myth, you know? What's the ongoing story? Where's it really going? So, you've got this schizophrenic attitude with the networks terrified of people tuning it out, and people who didn't see the first couple of episodes being unable to join mid-season, which is legitimate. But certainly people who want to join in this day and age can view the episodes on pay-per-view or streaming. There's many ways you can catch up on shows beyond just what airs. I think that the serialized fear is a bit overblown in the executive ranks, but it is real. It's something you've got to deal with.

KURT SUTTER, Showrunner: Sons of Anarchy

I know that as an artist I'm drawn not necessarily to violence or sexuality in terms of darker fare, but very serialized things. I'm drawn to things with deep mythologies, and it's really very difficult to do that on network. *Lost* was such an anomaly in broadcast, to have a show with such a deep mythology that you literally needed webisodes and an hour of qualifying videos by the showrunners to explain to the audience what was going on. It was wonderful and they handled it beautifully and it engaged you more in the process.

It's such an anomaly in [the broadcast] landscape, where people are so afraid to put something on the air that forces people to commit to a show. They're slaves to research that shows viewing audiences only watch a couple of episodes out of a series, and so everything is about being standalone. How do we break our creative process into enough pieces to service all this fucking research so we can somehow break the trend, or defy reality and have our cake and eat it too? They keep trying and they keep failing, and as a result of that I believe the quality of television in that area diminishes. It's the same thing that happened with the commercial and independent film industry years ago, when the independent film industry began to blossom because you had people that got so ass-ripped by the fucking studio system that they just fled to the independent arena. You had fantastic and wonderful projects come out of that, and I think that's what's happening in cable. You have the creatives and the people that have original voices that want the ability to explore and not necessarily have the chokehold of an accountant controlling which direction your pen moves in.

DAMON LINDELOF, SHOWRUNNER: LOST, THE LEFTOVERS

"Serialized" is a dirty word, and the irony is that it shouldn't be, because if you look at the top ten television shows and the shows that get nominated for Emmys and Golden Globes, they're all serialized, including reality shows. There's nothing more serialized then a reality show

I do feel like life is serialized. Life is not a procedural, and therefore that's the kind of storytelling that I like to watch, and it's the kind of storytelling that I like to write. That being said, I think that it's unfair to categorize shows as procedural or serialized, or as one working better than the other. I think that's what networks like to do, but at the end of the day, if you put something cool in front of them, they don't care whether it's a serialized or a procedural or a marriage of both. I think there are shows like *The Good Wife* now that are procedural shows but are actually stealth serialized shows, and that's why they are getting nominated for Emmys. If *The Good Wife* was just a show about Julianna Margulies in a courtroom every week putting bad guys away, or defending bad guys, it would not be nearly as interesting as the show that they've constructed, which is heavily serialized.

ROBERT KING, Showrunner: The Good Wife

We would agree that it's a bit of a wolf in sheep's clothing. There are certain elements that we have to satisfy to be on CBS, which is to be a show that has a story that we tell within the episode, and which has cases. It's partly that, and partly the characters that weave through it. It's not even trying to be cynical in an attempt to do that. Most people, when they're going through something terrible in their lives—a death, a divorce, some problem in their lives—they still have to go to work. So it's bit of a lie when it's a drama that doesn't have a story attached, because I don't care what's going on in our life, we have to come into work here and your emotional life affects how you work.

JONATHAN NOLAN, Showrunner: Person of Interest

I think we're in a very similar position to the Kings, and I think we took a similar approach, although we're very upfront and the network was always very supportive about the serialized component to the show. It never came up. It never became a thing of, "Oh, you can't do that," because, I think one of the reasons why we wanted to work with CBS was that the concept was a great fit for their network. I'm a big believer in "find the idea, figure that out, and then find the right home for that idea," because the idea driving our show was random access. The machine spits out a different number. You explore a different world every week. That's a creative choice on the part of the show. It just so happens to line up really nicely with the kinds of shows that CBS knows how to make really well. We knew that CBS was fantastic for making lots of stuff, but in particular procedural-based episodic crime shows. That, at essence, is how our show is like *The Good Wife*.

DEAN DEVLIN, Executive Producer: Leverage

At the time that we started [*Leverage*] the trend on TV was to do things that were very cold, procedural, dark, and edgy. I found those shows to be very compelling. I mean I enjoyed watching them, but I didn't want to live there—I didn't want to go and make that every week—that just wasn't going to be fun for me. So when I was asked what kind of show I wanted to do I was really thinking back to the shows I grew up on that I loved. Shows like *The Rockford Files* or *The A-Team*, or movies like *Ocean's 11*. I wanted to do something fun. Life is hard; entertainment should be fun. And so that's why we chose to go down this road.

JONATHAN NOLAN

The story that we wanted to tell is this larger, novel-like story that's similar to the shows that are flourishing right now on cable. I think the network knows the audience's tastes are changing. We never thought of the procedural as a four-letter word, and we've always embraced it. I grew up watching *Magnum, P.I., Miami Vice,* and *Hill Street Blues,* and all these amazing shows made by great writers and directors that had that self-contained story of the week to them. The shows that are flourishing right now are these serialized, novel-like shows on cable. Broadcast was always capable of doing both.

HART HANSON, SHOWRUNNER: BONES, THE FINDER, BACKSTROM

The network's appetite for *Bones* is very simple: as long as it's performing, they will want the show. On the creative side, there's an infinite number of murder stories, so our procedural part could go for ever. People are going to keep murdering each other, and we'll find ways of catching the murderer. That's the simple, but not the easy part, of the storytelling in *Bones*. The trickier part is keeping our audience interested in what's going on between our characters.

ANDREW MARLOWE

One of the virtues of a show like *Castle* being character-oriented is that our characters are growing. You can see from season one to now how Beckett is slowly opening up more and more and more. We like to talk about the Castle–Alexis relationship as if they're both growing up together. That change in points of view allows us to revisit some of the kinds of stuff we did in the first and second season, but with a new point of view so that it feels very much like a new show or a new perspective. That being said, we know with every change we make in the characters, every bit of growth, we always have to find a way for that growth to re-embrace the core values of the series, so the series doesn't change. This becomes particularly hard when you're in season four or five or six. If you start out with a character who's a fish out of water, by season four they're not a fish out of water anymore. One of the things we love about *Castle* in the beginning of the series is that he is giving us that outsider's perspective and he's not just another cop. We know now we have to be vigilant because he's been in the precinct, he's been hanging out with cops, but he's still finding a way to present us with an outsider's perspective to keep the show fresh and give Beckett and the boys something to react to.

HART HANSON

In our case, the minute [*Bones* lead] Emily [Deschanel] came to me and whispered in my ear that she was pregnant, which she very kindly did, very early—she let me know, I think, within five minutes—I said, "I know what to do. We'll just have Brennan be pregnant as well, and the world will not look the same. The two of them will have slept together, and there will be a baby." There are two disparate ways of looking at the world, and they will be in them together with the baby, and solving crimes. That gives a lot more stories. I felt like it just energized the series. It's a way of rebooting in a really good way.

ANDREW MARLOWE

Ghosts of the engine that you start the show with will remain, but sometimes you've got to put the car up on the block and rebuild the engine to get back to what you've been doing really well. When it feels like we're starting to peter out on that, I have a couple tricks up the sleeve to reinvent the show. But I would never look to blow up the fundamental values of the show because I think that's what people are tuning in for. Sometimes you actually have to change the show to get back to what you're doing really well, and back to the core identity of the show. If you don't do that, you end up drifting away from the kind of fun or the kind of storytelling or the kind of challenges that you've giving the audience every week.

RUNNING OUT OF STORY

The longer a show remains on the air, and depending how finite the premise of a show is, there comes a time on most shows where the writers begin scrambling to produce quality stories. Especially with one-hour dramas, the trend is to push along story at a break-neck speed to keep audiences engaged. A plot point or story-turn that writers used to hold back for a midseason-break episode, or a season finale, now gets used up, because of the story churn (think *Scandal*, *The Good Wife*, or *The Vampire Diaries*). Every showrunner handles it differently depending on the demands of their show.

As with all shows that get at least a 22-episode order, the darkest writing time comes in the winter. As *The Big Bang Theory*'s Bill Prady attests, "When you come back from a winter break and you start on the episodes that you're going to shoot—the January, February episodes—February is one of the worst times. You're exhausted and that wonderful cushion of scripts that you've built up in pre-production or that five, six, seven scripts you were ahead, that's gone. You're not ahead anymore at all. You're often finishing the script that's going to [table] read on Wednesday morning on Tuesday morning, and proofreading it while you're standing on the stage filming the episode on Tuesday night. It starts to feel like you're not going to make it.

For Damon Lindelof and Carlton Cuse, they had to

convince ABC to let them end *Lost* with a specific episode order they could write to while retaining quality. Lindelof explains: "Eventually the show reached this point where it just wasn't interesting to watch anymore. Your brain started telling you, 'They're stalling.' We literally, had to lock our characters in cages in order to prevent them from getting off the island. We'd been going to [former ABC Entertainment chief] Steve McPherson since the first season of the show, and in between the second and third season of the show, basically saying, 'Hey, we've got to end this thing.' They just didn't take us seriously. But then they were like, "These episodes aren't that good." We were like, 'We know. This is what we were telling you was going to happen. Wouldn't it have been great if we never had to make them in order to prove it to you?'

"At the end of the day, your ambition every time you're making an episode is for it to be the best episode you've ever made. The reality of the situation is, we're writing a script every ten days. The bar is very high. Also, the degree of difficulty was always very, very high to execute an episode of *Lost*. We began to realize, every episode is not going to be a home run. We started looking at the seasons as a whole, as opposed to an episode-by-episode analysis."

For a heist-dependent show like *Leverage*, the writing team had to create a crack case of burglary every script. John Rogers explains: "I don't think there's an alarm system we haven't hacked, even experimental stuff. We were going to security conferences and desperately finding new innovative ways that people try to lock other people out, so we can defeat it. We spent a lot of time trying to come up with perfect crimes. They have to be perfect and you must foil them because you have to be more perfect. It gets to be a bear. It really gets to be pretty monstrous. So the episodes came from three different places: it's something cool to steal, a cool villain that they hate, or a story they've always wanted to tell. We'd just throw those together and sometimes it's a villain from one writer and a thing from another. **"**

STAFFING A TV SERIES WRITERS' ROOM

O nce a creator/showrunner has made it through the nearly impossible gauntlet of getting their pilot picked up by a network, and everyone is on the same page about the show's structure and genre, then a showrunner can dig into the incredibly important task of building a writing staff for the show.

It's the rare Aaron Sorkins of the television world who are content writing the majority of their series episodes, with writing staffs serving essentially as draft and clean-up support. The majority of showrunners require a functional writing staff to help them brainstorm and break down episode ideas, create outlines, write scripts, complete rewrites, and, increasingly, produce on set when their script is in production.

As the showrunners have made it abundantly clear, they're overbooked every working day. A crack writing staff can sometimes make all the difference regarding whether a showrunner ever sees their home in the sunlight for nine months. It's imperative that a showrunner selects the right writers.

"The hardest thing about showrunning probably now is staffing and putting together the proper staff," showrunner Dee Johnson of *Nashville* reiterates. "That's a really difficult thing. It's a little "lightening in a bottle-esque" because it's such a recipe of personality types, talent, skill, and ability to take the punches. Those things sound simpler than they really are."

JEFF MELVOIN, SHOWRUNNER: ARMY WIVES

Hiring and firing a staff is one of the most critical things you can do as a showrunner. I don't think there's a lot of mystery about it. It's just a lot of homework. Even with the same showrunner, different shows have different demands.

DEE JOHNSON, Showrunner: Boss, Nashville

What I really look for is the total chemistry of a room and, of course, the ability to be a good writer. You read your samples and you respond to them, or you don't. Then you have to populate your room. It's a little bit like polling a jury, or putting a jury together. You want to make sure you have the right chemistry. One bad apple can derail a room.

When you are in the business long enough you can certainly do recon. You can call your friends and say, "Tell me about this person or that person or what your experience is like." But ultimately if you hire somebody, particularly at lower levels, it's a bit of a gamble. You are going to read a script, you'll interview, and some people interview great. It's a roll of the dice: hopefully they live up to it, sometimes they don't. I think that I've been really fortunate and I've worked with some really wonderful people. I haven't had too many crushing disappointments in that regard.

ANDREW MARLOWE, Showrunner: Castle

You know every writer has strengths and weaknesses, so putting together a team is little bit like putting together a sports team. If you have an organization that is filled with quarterbacks, you are going to be relatively dysfunctional and nobody is going to get along. It was finding team members and specific roles and that chemistry that you actually have to address every year. You have to change the formula a little bit just to keep the storytelling fresh, and make sure that people who are graduating to the next level of leadership aren't overweighting your organization at the top level, and that you are always bringing in your role players.

MIKE KELLEY, Showrunner: Swingtown, Revenge

I think that you hire people (at least I do) to start with based on the material that you read of theirs. I'm always inspired by their material and to meet them. If it's not a fit for your show, if a writer doesn't ultimately end up working out on your show, it's rarely because they don't have talent. It's really hard to get into somebody's rhythm, and somebody's voice.

MIKE ROYCE, Showrunner: Men of a Certain Age, Enlisted

When you're reading writers to work on your show, you look for tonal matches. It's hard, because sometimes you get a submission from someone who could be a great writer, but they've given you something that doesn't feel like the show we're doing. I have 150 scripts piled up on my desk. I can't read all those scripts. You have to be the dick whose reading 10 pages and going, "Well, no," even though it could be a very good pilot, because it just doesn't quite match. You don't have time to run down [and see] whether they have other stuff. Sometimes you do, but everybody can't get a fair shake, unfortunately.

JEFF MELVOIN

There's no one thing you're looking for in an interview. What I try to tell people when I interview them is that it's not a referendum on their ability. I've already decided I like your work, I think it's terrific. I'll often try to talk about their work, which is something I suggest other showrunners do too. It lets the interviewee be at ease and say, "Wow. This person really read me." They can talk about my work, and then I invite them to talk about what we're doing. I don't ask them to pitch, but I'm curious about what they think about the show, what they like about it particularly. We'll talk about any number of different things.

JOHN ROGERS, Showrunner: Leverage, The Librarians

You need to be taught how to write every show. So, if somebody comes in and they have a good general knowledge base and they seem to know the tone, we'll go with them. We've had a couple of people where they had never written this type of show before, but talking to them, you know that they'll do well at it.

CHRIS DOWNEY, Showrunner: Leverage

We have a good sense when we interview people whether they'll fit in, whether they seem like they have the right temperament for the room. It's a free flow of ideas, so you need to have a lot of energy in this room. You need to not get your feelings hurt if your idea doesn't get in.

STAFFING SEASON

Staffing season is the traditional period when broadcast series allow showrunners to hire writers for their writer rooms. Writer/producer Pam Davis explains:

“ Staffing season ends mid-May. When all the networks go to upfronts, they know what's coming back. They know what products are being picked up. You should've had all your meetings [by then] and if you haven't you're in trouble. If you don't have a job by May 17th to May 20th, then you might get picked up on a cable show in the fall, or you might sell a pilot in November-ish. Or you wait until the next staffing season, in April and May.

"Competition during staffing season is awful and terrible. I'm not positive how many one-hour drama writers in L.A. there are, but say there's 5,000 writers that are eligible? And I'm sure there's more. There's probably 1,200 positions a year open, if that, so it's really horribly competitive. But meetings are actually kind of fun; once you get them, the meetings are fun.

"If you don't get staffed on a show, particularly for a younger writer, you can be out in the cold until the next staffing season comes around," *Husbands* co-showrunner Jane Espenson continues. "I had that happen early in my career. I just didn't get staffed one year and it was very scary. There's nothing you can do but wait. Your agent tells you, 'Well, there'll be some mid-season staffing going on.' Then you're like, 'What? Can you get my stuff out there?' You're fighting with all the other people who have just gotten off shows that have been cancelled, so they're all back in the pool again swimming around with you. It can be very nerve-wracking. But, there are those mid-season shows, and there are more and more shows now like cable shows that staff up at weird times of the year. There's development. I'm at a level now where if I didn't get staffed some season, I'll go pitch pilots and maybe someone will want to buy one of those. That's no longer a scary proposition. 🟐🟐

JEFF MELVOIN

Per episode, you could have $50,000, or $60,000, or $80,000. You can spend it any way you want; you can get four $20,000 episode writers for $80,000, or maybe you can get one at that number and buy a number of younger people at $8,000–$10,000. It's all up to you. It's a little like *Moneyball*. I want to get the maximum bang for the buck. I do not want to overspend for people. I'd rather have more people in the room and have the opportunity to pick and choose.

MIKE ROYCE

A standard budget always sucks because you always want more writers. It's just a math game. You're paying for upper-level people; lower-level people don't cost as much. You have to try to work it out so that you're getting the people that you know have skills, plus the people who are new that you hope have skills. You need people who can be on the stage helping actually run things. You need great draft writers. You need great joke writers for comedy. You hope you get all those things in each person, but sometimes you're saying, "Well, this person's good at this, so then we'll use them more in this capacity." It's a lot of assessing that kind of stuff.

Working with Writers

In the creative sphere, the consideration and care for fellow artists is a huge factor in the success of any endeavor. By virtue of their title, showrunners are at the top of the writer chain of command and they set the standard for how healthy a writers' room is going to be.

Writers coming up through the system all have war stories about terrible rooms or bosses, but luckily there are just as many stories about great showrunners who have helped mold future writers' rooms away from being ground zero for potential therapy bills.

RONALD D. MOORE, SHOWRUNNER: BATTLESTAR GALACTICA, OUTLANDER

Ira Steven Behr on *Star Trek* and Jason Katims (*Friday Night Lights*) were similar men and similar mentors to me, in the sense that they both conducted themselves as the first among equals in the writers' room. They tried to let the best idea win. That was the most important thing. It wasn't important that they had the last word so much, as they found the best part of the story. I tried to take that away from the experience too.

TERENCE WINTER, SHOWRUNNER: BOARDWALK EMPIRE

The main thing that David [Chase] tried to impress upon us as writers was to always be entertaining. First and foremost we're putting on a television show and it's got to be entertaining to people, they have to be engaged and curious and wanting to come back next week. I actually have a sign in my own writers' room that just says, "Be entertaining." If you think about *The Sopranos*: it was funny, it was violent, there was great music, there was action, there was just a lot going on there. It was just something that you just always keep in mind. In terms of running the show, David had a great ability to just assemble a group of really talented people. We had an incredible crew and a really fun environment.

SHAWN RYAN, Showrunner: The Shield, The Unit

[*Nash Bridges*] was a great show to come up on and work on. Carlton [Cuse] was a real mentor. He was the boss who gave me my first steady TV gig. He would talk about how you weren't gonna make a career off of any one specific episode that you wrote, but if the show did well, we'd all do well together. What he meant by that was just because my name's not on this next script coming up, doesn't mean that it's not my responsibility to make that episode as good as it can be. And so I tried to carry that attitude on to *The Shield* with Kurt [Sutter], Glen [Mazzara], Scott [Rosenbaum], these guys who wrote on the show with me, let's not be competitive. If there's an episode that's not as good as the others, that's all of our faults. It doesn't matter whose name is on the script; we all are responsible for making each and every episode as good as it can be. So when you're sitting in that writers' room, you know you're not saving some idea for an episode of yours later on; if it can work now, you give it now.

STEVEN S. DEKNIGHT, Showrunner: Spartacus

One of the things that I learned from Joss Whedon when I worked with him—and I feel very honored that I got a chance to learn what it takes to run a show from a master like him—is that with each episode of his show there was a bigger, overarching story for the season. But each episode of the show had a beginning, middle, and end. And he always ended an episode so that even though it was close-ended, you couldn't wait to see what happened next week. And that's something that I really wanted to take [to *Spartacus*]. I wanted to take that almost moving serial 1940s kind of feel, and try it in each episode as strongly as possible, where you felt like something major just happened, and you had to know what happens next.

DEE JOHNSON, Showrunner: Boss, Nashville

There's been a bit of an auteur movement in television, which is a singularity of voice, meaning no one else really writes the show, people just sort of function as what we call "story monkeys," and everything goes through the showrunner's computer, and no one really writes. I think that's happened more and more and more, and that's not my cup of tea, but I have seen it happen a lot. That's sort of a short-term game, in my estimation anyway. You might get the singular vision and that is a brilliant thing, but when that show's over, who picks up the baton? That's why I go back to the John Wells (*E.R.*) "School of Showrunning." I think that there's something to be said for training, and for learning, and for helping and mentoring.

HOW TO NURTURE BABY WRITERS

The road to becoming a (semi) confident writer often comes with great mentoring and guidance, but the breakneck speed of television doesn't really allow for that luxury from a showrunner to all of his writers. However, that doesn't mean a showrunner has to throw teaching out the window all together. Mike Kelley talks about how he was mentored on *The O.C.* and continued that practice on *Revenge*.

Mike Kelley
" I know I struggled really hard on *The O.C.* It wasn't easy and it didn't come second nature. I did the best I could with it, and sometimes I did better than others. At the end of one of the seasons, [executive producer] Bob DeLaurentis says to me, he says, 'So Mike, you know, you could come back next year and you can write another person's show and you'll do well. You'll have a good career. You're a serviceable writer.' I'm just kind of like, 'Thanks.' He said, 'But what you should really do is quit and go write something that only you can write, in the voice that only you have. Tell a story that nobody

else can tell.' I said, 'Absolutely. Over hiatus. Can I just come back?' He said, 'That's not scary enough.'

In retrospect, he probably just fired me in the gentlest way he knew how. He was such a great mentor, and he was so kind. He was such a good teacher that what I learned from him is that you can't judge your writing based on whether or not you're a good mimic. I try to treat all of my writers with kindness and I try to treat them all with fairness. I try to be really encouraging. When I get a draft that isn't working, depending on how much time we have, I'm never thinking, 'This person's fired,' in my head, ever. I'm thinking, 'How can I help this person get the draft to a place that it needs to be sooner next time.'

Whether or not I sit down and give comprehensive notes, which is rarely, I will always give them my version of the script that they turned in, the draft that I've gone through, and say, 'Look at these two things and see where the changes are. See if you can get closer to this for next time.' Generally they do. It's incremental. Then you have the occasional person who just hits it out of the park. That's great, but it's really hard to do.

I think the more you nurture your writers, the more that you try to challenge them to hear your voice and think like you, the better it goes. Honestly, when I read somebody's material, even on a spec script, my favorite part is when they've added some imagination, some invention, some flare of their own. I go, 'Oh, that's great. I never would have thought of that. That's terrific stuff.' As long as the rest of it feels like the show, I just want writers to have some ownership of what they're doing. 〞

Lessons in Practice

A t the exit of every writers' room there is accumulated wisdom for every writer to put into action at the next job. If those writers eventually become showrunners themselves, there are myriad techniques that can be employed to get the best creative results from their staffs.

J.H. WYMAN, SHOWRUNNER: FRINGE, ALMOST HUMAN

I'm all for small rooms. I'm a quiet thinker. I like to consider things a lot. When you have a room of 12 or 15 people that are like, "And this or that," what it's great for is that you get a whole bunch of great ideas. They come and they're from anywhere. They run the gamut from being on-topic to off. Then you look at it and go, "I never would've thought of that," and that's great. What it also does is it derails you a lot of times because if you're really trying to chase the rabbit of what you're trying to say, you get a lot of different people who don't really want to chase the same rabbit. Then all of a sudden you become shapeless. It's my job as showrunner to say, "No. Wait guys. We need to focus on this." It's much easier to sit with the writers and actually just have two minutes of literal silence and just think about it. It's so much easier to stay on theme and everybody gets it. It's really become my favorite thing ever.

JAMES DUFF, SHOWRUNNER: THE CLOSER, MAJOR CRIMES

I remember telling [TNT EVP] Michael Wright when we first pitched the show, "Right now, you're only going to see the best I can do. Wait until I get into a room with seven really smart people, and then you can see how good the show can be with lots and lots of really smart people working at it," and that's what we've tried to do. We've tried to elevate the show every episode and we've hired people and we put together a team that's dedicated to that principle.

I think part of the reason why the writing staff hasn't changed is that the effort that every individual makes is recognized and appreciated. Everybody wants somebody to appreciate their contributions, and here, the writers are very much appreciated, not just by me—that would be natural, of course—but also by the actors and by post and by production. We are without hierarchy here, so that there are no factions and no separate camps.

ANDREW MARLOWE, Showrunner: Castle

When you're in the writers' room you never want to kill an idea in its infancy even if it seems ludicrous, because it can lead you to somewhere interesting. Oftentimes you can figure out a way to land it. We did an episode where we're living in the zombie world. It was something that we had wanted to do because zombies are very much in the zeitgeist and the challenge to us was how to deliver it credibly. Instead of saying, "There's no way to deliver zombies credibly, what are you guys, nuts?" It was, "Let's figure it out. Let's play with it." Somebody will come up with an idea that is incredibly off base, but like with improv, you want to be supportive of the idea and then see if it can land you somewhere better. The idea itself may be rubbish but it may lead to the conversation that gets you somewhere really beautiful and really interesting.

J.H. WYMAN

[On *Fringe*] we usually wrote in teams of two. Everybody contributed to everybody else's work. We like it where everybody feels that they're in a creative, safe place. They can actually not be laughed at, and not be ridiculed or scrutinized for an idea that may not go over well, but feel that they're in a very safe place, and they can say whatever their imagination sort of comes up with. That's how we get the best work out of people. That's really what it takes.

JOHN ROGERS, Showrunner: Leverage, The Librarians

The best thing for me is being in the writers' room. It's not even when the story is broken; it's that moment when actually you can lean back and the room's momentum is already carrying it. It's like, "Oh, this story is so good, I could step in front of a bus right now and this would just keep going. They'd finish writing before they'd pick me up off the street." When I was in stand-up, I used to say that the cool thing was not getting the laughs, it's the moment that you do the set up to a joke, and you pause, and everyone in the room leans forward. And *then* you do the joke. It's the same thing in the room. The story is great, but for me, the really great bit is when everyone is totally engaged and they are thinking about nothing else but this really cool idea. It's a communal creativity that you don't see in a lot of other places.

BILL PRADY, Showrunner: The Big Bang Theory

If you start thinking about the episodes that you're going to do next year, or the episodes that you're going to do for the next three years… they'll cart you away into a room and feed you soft food for the rest of your life. That's the end of it. You have to develop this tunnel vision where you're looking at this episode or this scene or this joke or this moment. You have to develop the ability to live in the micro and not in the macro. One of the interesting things about the approach that we've taken at *The Big Bang Theory*, and this was always strongly encouraged by [co-creator] Chuck Lorre, is to not plan, to not develop story arcs that last over the season or over multiple seasons, or even to fiercely protect the ending you imagine in the episode that you're writing. Chuck says, "You're writing toward an ending." The great advantage of it is you know what the episodes are going to be.

ANDREW MARLOWE

The interesting thing to me about television is that you can create this ongoing conversation with the culture. If you're successful and you're on for thirteen episodes or two seasons or four seasons or eight seasons, you really have a chance to develop characters over time and you really get a chance to see what your impact is on the audience. I think those evolutionary pressures make the job difficult but also really exciting because you can't rest on your laurels these days. You always have to be pushing your storytelling into new territory. You can't just say, "Okay. I have an audience. I'm going to cruise for a season or two." You always have to be continuing to think: how you are going to build that audience? How are you going to challenge the audience so they don't get bored? How are you going to do new storytelling?

JOSS WHEDON, Showrunner: Buffy the Vampire Slayer, Firefly, Dollhouse

The amount of procrastination in the writers' room can become eventually absurd and toxic, where we are not able to stay on point and thinking that we needed this absurd flow of just jokes and dirty stories and talking about our personal lives, ultimately lead to a lot of longer hours than they should have, and that's not helping anybody. Because of my fear of conflict, I tend not to communicate with people when they're doing something right or wrong. [Executive producer] David Greenwalt, who is one of the meaner people I've ever known, God bless him, had to explain to me that I should tell people that they were doing a good job. My response to which was, "Well, I didn't fire them so clearly they're doing a good job." He said, "No, it's more than that, do it." At the same time, if someone was doing a bad job, I don't know how to tell them. What would happen is if we needed to fire somebody, or if they needed to be uprooted, it was coming out of nowhere and they would go, "What's going on, what do you mean?" I had to learn to keep that focus on the whole picture and that communication and looking at the minutiae, as well and making sure that everybody is co-operating and everybody understands where we're going.

TERENCE WINTER

Once we have a pretty good idea where we want to go [for a season], we sit down and go: what happens in episode one and what's the story in there? How do we hit these points along the way? It's a lot of discussion. It's probably a six to eight week period of just talking before we even generate an outline. Once we have an outline that we all do in the room, it's basically 25 to 33 beats, each one of those beats being a scene. It's all written down on a board and once we get the outline, we'll move on. We'll try to create enough outline so every writer or writing team will have their own episode. Ideally, we generate five outlines and then we take off two weeks to write. I'm in the writers' room exclusively for the first couple of months before we're in production.

ALI LeROI, SHOWRUNNER: *EVERYBODY HATES CHRIS*, *ARE WE THERE YET?*

When we were in the run for *Are We There Yet?*, we had eight weeks of pre-production and I only had four staff writers and a small group of freelancers that I would work with. The traditional sitcom writers'-room way of approaching the material didn't work for me. It may work for some others, but for me it didn't work. Creatively we like to keep the train moving. Someone comes in with an idea, I say, "I like that idea. Give me a page of beats on how you think the story will work." Then I can have three or four people doing that. It was challenging, I think, and rewarding for the writers because on a normal sitcom with 12 writers on staff and only 20 episodes to do, you might get one or two episodes maybe in a season. With 90 to do and four people on staff, guess what? You're going to get a lot of scripts. You can get as many as you can write. It's all about if the story makes sense, if I can get down 40 pages of something that's linear that makes sense. I can make it funny. I can punch it up.

JOSS WHEDON

I think the philosophy of my room for the writers has always been, "fall in love with moments, not moves." It was the essence of everything, which was that every show needs to have a separate intent. It doesn't have to be moral. It doesn't have to be anything but intent; just this one little thing. A move is, "Oh my God! It was his evil twin!" Evil twin gives you nothing, unless there is some extremely relatable thing that everybody has gone through in regards to an evil twin that you can mine, and that's your moment. We will protect moments at all cost. I will give up a good move in a heartbeat. It's very hard. Most writers are taught, "Just keep it going until you get to the end. Whew, we got through another one, and then shoot out in the warehouse." Believe me, I've done my share of shoot-outs in warehouses, I'm sorry to say. For us, it's always got to be, what do we need to see? Where's the big movie moment, whether it's emotion, whether it's funny, whether it's action? What's that thing we're leading up to that hits you in the heart? Very often you can think you have one and then realize it's a move disguised as a moment, or vice versa.

IN DEPTH:

COMING UP *THE SOPRANOS* WAY WITH TERENCE WINTER

Until his late twenties, Terence Winter harbored a deep secret that he never shared with the world: that he wanted to be a television writer. Kids from Brooklyn didn't chase such weird dreams, so instead he pursued vocational and retail jobs until he decided to go to college. It was there he was encouraged to pursue his real dreams, and got into the business of writing for shows like *The Cosby Mysteries* and *Xena: Warrior Princess*. His eventual home, where he learned the skills that prepared him to create *Boardwalk Empire*, was HBO's *The Sopranos*. How does a New York guy get made in a show about the New Jersey mob?

TERENCE WINTER

I had been bouncing back and forth between sitcoms and dramas in my career, and I had no real career path planned out. My career strategy was: if you offered me a job, I would take it. You look at my resume and it's just all over the place, I don't think you could figure out what I was doing.

My agent at the time called me up, he said, "I have this pilot episode of a show called *The Sopranos* I want you to watch, and I'm going to send it to you." Like everybody else in the world, I thought it was opera based. I thought, "Why me?" He goes, "Just watch it."

I don't think I even finished watching it and I was trembling. I said, "This is the greatest thing I've ever seen." I called my agent, I said, "You've got to get me on this show." He said, "Yeah, well, you know…" I said, "No, no. You have *got* to get me on this show. I can write this show." I grew up in a neighborhood that had guys like that in it, and I knew these people. I understood the culture, I understood the psychology.

My second call was to a guy named Frank Renzulli, who co-created the first show I ever worked on, *The Great Defender*. Frank grew up in Boston in a similar environment and I said, "Have you seen this thing, *The Sopranos*?" He said, "Yeah, I'm actually meeting with this guy David Chase on Friday." I said, "You got to get me in there with you." He said, "All right, I'll do my best."

As it turned out, David had already hired his whole first year staff, so I kind of sat out on the sidelines during season one. What David didn't know at the time was that Frank was sending me early drafts of all the scripts and I was doing some editing for him. We would talk about stories, so I was kind of in the writers' room but not in the writers' room. Frank would call me at the end of the day and tell me how it went and what stories they were working on, so I was just really on the sidelines.

Around the time, I had written a spec movie script called *Brooklyn Rules*, which kind of had a mob element. I thought, "Oh, this would be a great sample for David." I gave it to Frank to give to David as a sample, and David read it and hated it. It was like my big master plan just blew up in my face. I was like, "You're kidding me?" He goes, "No, he just doesn't like it." I said, "Shit, I just completely blew this."

Finally, season two came along and David had jettisoned most of the writers from the first season and kept Frank Renzulli, Robin Green, and Mitch Burgess, so he's looking to add some more writers. Finally, David said, "All right, who's this guy you've been telling me about. Are you sure he can write this show?" Frank said, "Absolutely, just give him a chance and I promise you."

Frank had no idea if I could write the show, but he was a good friend. David gave me an opportunity to write a script, and it was basically a trial thing that if it turned out, there might be an opportunity to be on staff. It went well. It was the fifth episode of the second season called 'Big Girls Don't Cry' and he liked it enough to hire me, and then the rest was history.

Working on *The Sopranos*—and I've said this to David many times—no matter what else I do in my career, that will be the experience that I compare everything else to. Not in a way that I'm setting out to try to top it or do something better. It was just a golden time for all of us, I think. Again it doesn't have anything to do with how successful anything was, it was just such a magical time that I don't think will ever be replicated. It just was lightning in a bottle in so many different ways. The people we worked with, the way the audience responded, the act of doing the actual work. The fact that we were so proud of what we were doing. It was just great, and it was just such a period in my life that I'll always look back fondly on, no matter what I do. God willing, I'll be on things I'm equally proud of or successful, but that was just absolutely magic for many, many years of my life."

CHAPTER THREE

HOW I GOT MY FOOT IN THE DOOR

Starting Out

There's no sense sugarcoating it: the opportunities for a newbie writer getting their foot in the writers' room door can be few and very far between. Writers' room production assistant or writer assistant gigs are rare, so there's fierce competition to snag one. Also, getting your writing read by people who can help foster it is another adventure all on its own. But the good news is that everyone that eventually gets hired as a writer had to come up the ladder like everyone else. Plus there's no fixed path for it to happen. Are there any inside tips to attaining that proverbial brass ring?

To put it simply: write often, rewrite, rinse, repeat.

Add persistence and networking and you have a better shot at hitting your goal career. To illustrate from personal experience, these showrunners share their stories on how they kept up their spirits and determination to finally break into the writers' circle.

RONALD D. MOORE, SHOWRUNNER: BATTLESTAR GALACTICA, OUTLANDER

I don't know if I was disheartened in the interim before I sold the first spec [an original script based on an existing series]. I think I was just confused. I didn't really know what I was doing and I started and stopped various scripts. My friend and I co-wrote a feature spec together once. I spec'd out a *Cheers* script and started various other features, but never finished them. I kind of bopped around from odd job to odd job, telling myself I'm here to be a writer and started working at New World International in their sales department and servicing. Somebody would sell a movie to Taiwan and I would be the guy who would actually send them the print and publicity materials and make sure the money was gotten in return. So I was sort of in the business, that was as close as I was to being in the business, and I went through periods where I thought I'm never going to do this, or that this is ridiculous.

Then I started dating this girl who found out that I was a huge fan of the original *Star Trek* series. She had worked at *Star Trek: The Next Generation* and had helped to cast the pilot, so she still had a couple of contacts over there. She said, "You know, I could probably get you a tour of the sets," because they had regularly scheduled set tours in those days as so many people wanted to go visit the *Star Trek* sets. I said, "Oh God, that'd be amazing," and "please, please, please make the call." So she made a call and sure enough got me onto a set tour. It turns out in retrospect that was the key moment of my career because I just decided what the hell, I'm going to write a spec script for a *Star Trek: The Next Generation* episode and take it with me, which was very atypical for me. I wasn't the guy that was knocking on people's doors and walking into offices with scripts. I was much lazier than that, but somehow the actual visit to the *Trek* set focused me and I decided I was going to do this.

I sat down and wrote a spec script called "The Bonding" and I brought it with me when they gave me the set tour. There was this young man who was giving me the tour and I conned him into reading it; he was one of Gene Roddenberry's assistants. He gave it to the woman that became my first agent. She submitted it to the show formally and it sat in a slush pile for about seven months. At the beginning of the third season a new executive producer came on board, the late Michael Piller, who started going through the slush pile looking for scripts and he found my script, bought it and asked me to write another one. I wrote a second one and then shortly after that he let go a writer on the staff and I got this call one day just saying, "I need a staff writer, can you start working tomorrow?" I said yes, and I was there ten years.

DAMON LINDELOF, SHOWRUNNER: LOST, THE LEFTOVERS

My first paying job, after doing a couple of internships, was working for an agency. I knew that they were the middlemen for all business. So, if I eventually wanted to be a writer, and agents represented writers and sold writers' work to studios, I felt like it would be a good idea to understand what it was that made agents sign people in the first place. I looked at LA as my grad school. I approached it as,

"Well, I have to have talent, so I don't know whether I have that or not, but let's assume for argument's sake that I do, how do I market myself as a commodity?"

I got a year of completely and totally irrelevant business experience. Then once I understood how the agencies worked, I moved on to the studios. I wanted to see what the buyers thought. From their perspective, what was a marketable movie and who were writers that they wanted to work with over and over again? I did that for a year at Paramount, where I read a lot of scripts. My boss, a guy by the name of Michael Hackett, was a creative executive there. His job was to, essentially, read around 25 scripts a week; that's two or three scripts a day. Every weekend, we'd send home this thing called "weekend read." I probably spent 10,000 hours just reading scripts over the course of the four years that I spent at Paramount, one year working for an executive, then the following three years working as a creative executive for a producer.

By the time I had gone through my five years of post-graduate work and now understood how the business was, I said, "Maybe it's time for me to make a go of it as a writer." So, I emailed everybody that I knew and said, "I want to quit my job as an executive. I know that I want to be a writer, but I can't make that leap yet. I'll be a writer's assistant. I'll get their coffee. I'll do their dry-cleaning. I'll wash their cars. Just get my foot in the door and I'll do the rest." One thing led to another and I was successful in beginning to develop my TV writer career.

JANET TAMARO, SHOWRUNNER: RIZZOLI AND ISLES

I never thought I'd be writing television. I loved being a journalist. It was like getting shot out of a cannon almost every day, chasing the next story, traveling to a different part of the country all the time. But what I loved about journalism is what eventually also repelled me from it. I have two children, and I was on the road all the time. It also became far more troubling to cover tragedies and crimes. That body on the ground doesn't get back up. It got to be relentless and profoundly disturbing.

I was in the ABC newsroom when the Oklahoma bombing happened, and I had a year-old baby girl. All of those in the newsroom who had children, we put our heads on our desks. It was the first time I remember thinking, "Please don't make me cover this." We were watching live images of dead children getting pulled from the wreckage. But it was my job. And I did it. Then one day, when I was covering a school shooting, I just decided, "I can't do this anymore."

The very first script I wrote was a freelance episode for what was then a new show. On a lark, I pitched a story to *Law and Order: SVU* and then wrote the script. When I say a lark, it wasn't, "Whoo-hoo, this is fun!" It was, "This is different. This is really challenging. Is this something I really want to do?" It is very challenging to write a script, and each and every time I face that page, I think, "This has got to get easier." If only… But with that very first script, a whole new world opened up for me. I thought, "I'm not bad at this, and this is absorbing and challenging. I get to fictionalize all these things that I've seen." I happened to be in New York when they shot that episode. I visited the set—and I had this big, stupid grin on my face when this cute little 22-year-old actress, who was playing a junkie, got shot—and then got back up. The director said, "Okay, let's do another take." That's when I knew I'd found my second profession.

DAVID SHORE, Showrunner: House

I was a lawyer and I had a friend that was out in LA writing, and I decided if I didn't give it a shot then I was never going to give it a shot. I also figured I'd come out here for two years and if I fell flat on my face it would just be an interesting story to tell people years later. I had no paid work for two years after I first came out here. I holed up in an apartment with my savings and started writing—trying to write. It's a tough business to break into. It is. I would send my stuff out and it took me about a year to get an agent, and it took me about a year after that to get an assignment, and then a year after that to get a second job. In hindsight, I'm thrilled with that progress.

My first job was a CBS show called *Due South*, which was not a legal show. Then I did another show up in Canada which was also not a legal show. I came back here and got on legal shows and I'm sure I got on them to a greater or lesser extent because of my legal background, and that worried me a little bit. I didn't want to be known as a lawyer who could write a little. I wanted to be known as a writer. I specifically didn't want to create a legal show when it came time for *House*. I'm not sure I wanted to create a medical show, but I specifically didn't want to create a legal show.

MIKE KELLEY, SHOWRUNNER: REVENGE

As an assistant, I worked on a number of failed endeavors. I started my training ground at Warner Brothers on a show called *Charlie Grace*. Bob Singer produced it. It's actually funny, I was going to leave town and go back to Chicago and throw in the towel the night before I got a job on that show as the script coordinator, which is a really important job in the life of a series. I had no idea how to do it. This girl at the bar, as I was sitting there sort of drowning my sorrows for free because it was the only way I could do it at the time, said, "What's wrong?" I said, "I'm just leaving town tomorrow." She said, "Why?" I said, "I couldn't make a go of it." She said, "So you want to be a writer?" I said, "Yeah." She said, "Listen, I'm the script coordinator on *Lois and Clark* and I happen to know that the producers are looking for a script coordinator for *Charlie Grace*." I said, "I have no idea how to do that job." She said, "You will by morning."

I went in and she said, "He's the best script coordinator in town, give him the job." I learned from there about how to write television. As a script coordinator all the drafts go through your computer; every revision, everything from the writer's first pass through to the showrunner's final polish. You learn a lot very quickly.

After I wrote a spec script for *Providence*, I was invited to come on the staff as a staff writer, and there are steps in between. Frankly, if you're lucky, you get to take each step along the way, and I did from assistant all the way through to where I am now as an executive producer. You start as a staff writer, then you go to story editor, and then executive story editor, and co-producer, and producer, and supervising producer, and co-ep, and then executive producer on the show if you get a show. For me, every one of those steps is important. You learn something new and the responsibilities get a little bit greater.

PAM DAVIS, PRODUCER: INTELLIGENCE

If you go back way back in time, in university I wrote a children's book, so I did a little publishing. I did a little magazine editing. When I was doing a magazine, I ended up at the Toronto Film Festival and somebody at the festival was doing a TV show, so I ended up doing TV and getting involved with more film and film financing. Then I met people who were going down to LA so I would visit them. At which point I met the Canadian Mafia down here, which is basically that all Canadians seem to introduce each other to everybody else. I bothered David Shore long enough and he said, "Come pitch me," and I got to do a freelance on one of his shows, called *Family Law*. Then when he created *House*, he asked if I wanted to be part of it.

STEVEN S. DEKNIGHT, SHOWRUNNER: SPARTACUS

I wanted to be an actor, and then I realized I wasn't tall enough or talented enough to actually be a successful actor, so I switched to playwriting and then I went to UCLA for my grad work as a playwright. I spent an extra year going through the screen-writing program at UCLA, because I decided I really wanted to write movies. Then I graduated, and I thought in six months to a year I'll get my career going and break in. During that time I got a job teaching English as a second language at a Japanese school in Van Nuys, and it was a great job.

Six and a half years later I could not get arrested. Everything I tried, nothing happened. I could not get any traction in features, and those were the dark days. I was living in a second-floor apartment in Glendale with no air conditioner. I was writing spec scripts—I'd work all day and then I'd come home and work on my writing. In the summer it was so hot I actually had to type naked because there was no air conditioning. My friends were all worried they'd find me electrocuted because I was sweating into the keyboard. It was hellish, literally hellish! But I kept plugging away, I kept plugging away, and then I thought, "Well, I watch a lot of TV and I love television so maybe I should, just as an exercise, write a spec TV script."

I was watching *Deep Space Nine* at the time so I wrote a *Deep Space Nine* spec about a giant Ferengi. Basically, Ferengi are dwarf-sized, so it was all about why Ferengis are small, which I sympathize with! I did this as an exercise, but nobody wanted to read it. Agents didn't want to read it, *Deep Space Nine* didn't want to read it and they accepted everything, so I just put it in a drawer. About a year later a buddy of mine that I went to school with, Delroy Robinson, calls me up and says, "Hey, I'm coordinating this MTV show that's created by Roland Joffé from *The Killing Fields*. It's absolutely horrible, it will never get on the air, but if they pick it up I can get your stuff to Roland Joffé's people." I go "Great," and I completely forget about it.

Four months later he calls me up and says, "I don't know how it happened, but they picked us up. Send me something." I sent him this *Deep Space Nine* script, which is the only television script I had. So he sends it to Roland Joffé's people and the guy that reads it is a huge *Deep Space Nine* fan. It's that kind of coincidence and happenstances that are career builders, and that's how I got my first job, doing *Undressed*. After four seasons, which is kind of like dog years, we had like 140 half-hour episodes in that period of time.

I decided to get a higher-profile agent to try to get off this show and get a mainstream network show. Again I took my favorite show on TV at the time, *Buffy The Vampire Slayer*, and I wrote a spec about it called "Xander the Slayer." It was about why men can't be slayers; basically, it goes to our heads and we become uncontrollable. It got into Joss Whedon's people's hands and I had a meeting with them, not with Joss but with his people, about coming on for the animated TV show they were trying to get off the ground. They said Joss has to read the script, and I spent the next, I think, eight weeks chewing my nails, and then I finally got a call that said, "Joss Whedon wants to see you." It's like being summoned by the Pope. And that was really when I felt like I think my career had really started: once I had worked with Joss on two seasons of *Buffy*, and then two seasons on *Angel*. He also gave me my directing chance and started my directing career.

ALI LeROI, Showrunner: Everybody Hates Chris, Are We There Yet?

My route to television writing was circuitous. I actually started out in sketch comedy a number of years ago and then I became a stand-up. While I was doing stand-up, I toured for a number of years with Bernie Mac. After I got off the road with Bernie, I went to New York to work with Chris Rock on his HBO show, and that's when I became a full-time writer. That was a choice: keep doing stand-up or write. They're both full-time jobs. I had a wife and a kid, and I couldn't be in both places. For me, it was a very practical choice. For me, it just felt like a more reasonable way to take advantage of my skill set and have a living and take care of my family. It's a glorified factory job.

JAMES DUFF, Showrunner: The Closer, Major Crimes

I started out writing plays, and I had a play on Broadway in my late 20s. That play went around the world, and then I had another play in New York. While I was writing that other play, I got offered a TV movie. After turning it down a few times, I finally said okay. Then, instantly, you're a television writer. I had never even actually read a TV movie before I wrote the TV movie I did for Fox, called *Daytime on Maple Drive*. I had to go and find TV movies and see what the format looked like and sort of play with the format for a while as I was doing it. I went from writing TV movies to staffing television shows. In the interim of doing all of that, I also wrote about 15 pilots for TV series and made four of them, which were so good I guess they decided not to go on and make them into series.

IN DEPTH:

WOMEN AND MINORITY SHOWRUNNERS

I t's no secret that the showrunner position is one largely dominated by white males. Despite the expansion of scripted programming into streaming services, premium cable, basic cable and now gaming console providers, that hasn't translated into an equally pervasive inclusion of minority voices as creator/ showrunners. In fact, according to the WGAW 2013 TV Staffing Brief, minorities (representing the cumulative categories of gender, race and age) only comprise 15.6% of employed television writers. What that means is that minorities, as a combined group, remain underrepresented by a factor of more than 2 to 1 in television staff employment, well below the average number of minorities (36% as of 2010) who populate the United States.

Breaking the numbers down more specifically regarding gender, the 2012-2013 Center for the Study of Women in Television and Film annual report by San Diego State University found women were making gains accounting for 34% of television writers and 27% of producers, but only 24% of series creators. With gains steadfastly remaining in the single digits since 1997 (when the study first began), the question remains why are minorities in general not getting opportunities? Why aren't studios and networks amping up their efforts to level the playing field with more women and ethnicities that represent a large percentage of their viewing audiences?

Showrunners Dee Johnson (*Boss, Nashville*), Janet Tamaro (*Rizzoli & Isles*) and Ali LeRoi (*Everybody Hates Chris*) all have their own theories and personal experiences that they share about what's not happening in the industry to include more diversity within the showrunner circle.

DEE JOHNSON

WHY DO YOU THINK WOMEN AREN'T GETTING SHOWRUNNER JOBS IN MORE COMPETITIVE NUMBERS TO THEIR MALE COUNTERPARTS?

I have so many theories about this. First off, it's really hard. I think culturally it's difficult just across the board. I think some people feel more comfortable with a guy at the helm. I don't know. I think there is just a comfort factor there societally. I think that's one part of it. The other part of it, and I joke with friends of mine who are also women in the business, is that there is something about the tenor of a woman's voice that makes it easier to ignore sometimes.

I have a little cartoon on my wall that shows a boardroom with all men and there is one woman and she has stood up and made a presentation. The chairman says, "That's a fantastic idea, Ms. Tripp. Perhaps one of the men should suggest it."

HOW HAVE YOU SEEN THAT GENDER DISPARITY PLAY OUT IN WRITERS' ROOM?

What happens so often in a room—and this isn't really just specific to women— is a no-win situation where she will pitch an idea out and it just hovers. Two minutes later that same idea will be jumped on by somebody else, a male, and typically it will be, "That's it, that's the idea!" There you are either left with the, "Hey, that was my idea." To which they will just go, "Oh, do you want credit, Dee?" Or you just sit there and take your lumps, which is usually what I will opt for. I think it's difficult to be heard sometimes and to be taken seriously without getting pushed to the, "I'm going to go nuclear bitch level" which is a very unpleasant place to stay.

ARE YOU SEEING MORE FEMALE WRITERS?

I know a lot of female writers. But what's odd also about the business—and this is probably my one big pet peeve and I wouldn't care so much if there was equity—but there are a lot of shows where the central characters are all women. But if you look at everybody from the top down, all the EPs, the writers, the directors it's all men, so their voice is never ever true. I have a friend who I have always joked with about creating a show that's about all guys and it's made by female directors and all female writers on staff. 'Let's do that!'

WHAT COMMON BIAS BOTHERS YOU?

There is a question that comes up more often for women which is can she write a man? I never hear anybody ask that about men being able to write women. I think that's one little element, not to bang the sexist drum, but it comes into play in life.

JANET TAMARO

WHAT COMPELLED YOU TO CREATE A FEMALE-CENTRIC DRAMA?

Frankly, I never said to myself, "I'm creating a 'female-centric drama.'" But I did have a strong desire to create characters who were fully-realized, powerful, smart, complex and contradictory—like the real women I know and admire. I didn't want my two female leads' lives to revolve around men, and I wanted to be able to depict real conflict between them. The first time I wrote a scene in which they disagreed, I got a "no cat fights" note. Really? Women don't have the right to argue? And if they do, we demean them with that dated term? I said, "Let's just try it." We shot it. It was funny and painful and real. After that, everyone was on board. "Yeah! More arguments."

DO YOU FEEL THE WEIGHT OF BEING A MINORITY SHOWRUNNER?

Okay, how weird is it that we're 51% of the population—and still a minority in so many professions? There are not enough women running shows. There are not enough women (or minorities) writing, producing and directing television and film and that's a real shame. My mother was seen as a freak when I was growing up because she had four kids—then went to law school. I'm sad to think she'd be an anomaly today. There should be more of us doing this job.

DO YOU PONDER THE REASONS WHY?

All the time. Right now, the industry doesn't have enough women in powerful positions or enough people from varied backgrounds, cultures and ethnicities. If we widened the circle, we'd have more stories to choose from, and the industry would be less likely to create programs that reflect a specific cultural bias.

WHAT ABOUT *RIZZOLI & ISLES* IS UNIQUE IN ITS CHARACTERIZATION OF WOMEN?

I don't know how "unique" it is, but I suspect, given how beloved Jane (Rizzoli) and Maura (Isles) have become, their friendship with each other hit a sweet spot. I hear from women all the time who tell me how "real" their relationship with each other feels. My goal was to go beyond a two-dimensional story of an odd couple friendship. I wanted them to be unapologetic about who they are, unafraid to be complicated and yes, contradictory. Bust a few stereotypes. Women are so much more interesting and so much more varied in real life than the ones we all too often see depicted on TV.

DOES BEING A FEMALE SHOWRUNNER PUT YOU AT A DISADVANTAGE?

I think whether you're male or female, being a showrunner is a hard gig. I had a conversation with a male executive producer who said, "I don't see any difference between the way men are treated and the way women are treated." I said, "Have you ever been a woman?" I can't really know what it's like to be a man, or to be another race or ethnicity. It's been my experience that some people—both male and female—have an easier time being told what to do by a man. But I'll be curious to see what happens when I run my next show. First-time showrunners are at a disadvantage because it's such a steep learning curve, regardless of gender. Every showrunner faces crushing demands: you must have a strong vision and voice, be decisive, stay on budget, write quickly and well, keep the three-ring circus performing and lead the troops. You have to fire people as well as hire them. You have to let writers know when they're not pulling their weight or missing the mark. Bottom line: you're supposed to be this wonderful creative genius, churn out pages, keep track of the budget and take care of everyone. There has been plenty of research documenting the double standard we have for our leaders. Identical behavior by a male and female boss often get perceived differently. Politicians, CEOs, military leaders are still mostly men. Things change slowly. So, he might be seen as a "forceful, dynamic, tough leader" while she's seen as "pushy and bitchy." That's too bad. But I think it's changing. The more women who rise to positions of power, the less being a female leader will be an issue. But whether you're a boy a girl, it's a hell of a lot easier to criticize a boss than to be a boss.

WHAT DO YOU THINK CAN HELP SHIFT THE PLAYING FIELD IN A BETTER DIRECTION?

When you first get your foot in the door, all you're thinking about is am I going to get the rest of my body in or am I about to lose that foot? But once you've done that—created a show and run it successfully, you have the opportunity to champion voices that may not have been heard. I hear too often that there just aren't enough good female writers or directors or showrunners. It takes experience and it takes time. But it first takes getting your foot in that door. You need 10,000 hours. You can't get great at something unless you've had the opportunity to do it over and over. We have to create those opportunities.

ALI LEROI
WHAT DO YOU SEE AS PART OF THE ISSUE WITH GETTING MORE MINORITIES INTO SHOWRUNNER POSITIONS?

Part of the process of becoming anything where one group of people are in charge and are left to choose who else is going to be a part of the thing, the onus is put on the people who were trying to get in to prove that they belong. People tend not to be generous about that sort of thing. You know there aren't a lot of black basketball players in the NBA because the white guys are just generous. The guys that got in were better than the rest of them. They're like, "Damn, these guys are good. This is amazing. I guess we've got to let them in."

Then over time things kind of balanced out like in the NFL. Now there's some mediocre black coaches, as there should be because there's lots of mediocre white coaches. Ideally, it would get to that point [in TV]. [Right now] the first brigade of whoever the minority is, like in the first group of women is Tina Fey who is brilliant because she has to be. Of course, Lena Dunham is brilliant. She has to be. Whatever people might think about me one way or another, I'm good at this. I have to be.

DOES SOMEONE LIKE SHONDA RHIMES' (GREY'S ANATOMY, SCANDAL) SUCCESS CREATE A DIFFICULT MODEL TO ATTAIN?

The tricky part about someone like Shonda Rhimes being successful is that again, she's extraordinarily talented, off the charts, so it's not really fair to compare the rest of the mere mortal women writers to Shonda Rhimes, as it's not fair to compare the rest of the female comedy writers to Tina Fey. She's off the charts brilliant. Where are the people who are just going to create sort of a middling, procedural drama? "Hey, we got a doctor show. It's nothing new or brilliant that you haven't seen before, but we think it'll work. Let's get a woman to run that show," or she came in and pitched something.

Again, when you take the best people and you use them as the examples of why, whoever the theoretically lesser people should be let into the building, it's kind of an unfair charge. You know, you've got (All-Star Los Angeles Lakers basketball player) Kobe Bryant on the team, and then you've got 11 other guys, but you need the 11 other guys. You need them, because Kobe Bryant can't produce all the points. And at some point he's not as good as he used to be, so it's the same thing. I'm sure Shonda is cultivating relationships and perhaps she's mentoring.

SHOULD THERE BE AN OBLIGATION BY MINORITY SHOWRUNNERS TO BRING UP THE NEXT GENERATION?

I've actually sat with [Shonda] and thought about trying to come up with some things, but it shouldn't really be about her having to mentor just female African American writers. Why should she be saddled with that? Why can't she just try and come up with what she thinks is good and what she thinks is dramatic and what she thinks will be entertaining, and then have those people who are likeminded work with her?

The only problem, if there is a gender or a racially based component to who gets let into the room, it's the decision makers who are in the studio position or in the network position believing somehow that because you're a woman, you can't write a cop show because it's action, or if you're a black guy, you can't work with Drew Carey because he's a white guy.

WHAT'S KEEPING THE MINORITY NUMBERS SO LOW?

Well, the thing about Hollywood is that the people who are in charge in the truest sense of the word—en masse—there are a few in particular who are risk-takers. There's a few. Most are not. Most have absolutely no idea what will work or why, so what they try to do is create something that's kind of like something else that worked. Marc Cherry didn't get *Desperate Housewives* on because he created some other brilliant serial comic soap. They didn't know. They were like, "Oh, that guy's a washed up sitcom writer." Yeah, and then he came up with something else. In his own way, he ran up against the same thing. He wasn't fitting into the box that they expected him to be in, so, "No, we don't want you to do that. Yeah Ali, when we've got a black guy we'll call you."

DO YOU HAVE AN EXAMPLE OF ETHNIC BIAS THAT CAME UP WITH YOUR CREATOR-BASED PROJECTS?

As a writer, I like to write. I write comedy, I write single cam stuff, multi cam stuff. I've done features. I've written dramas. I had a project that I was working on that I was talking to some executives about. As I pitched them the idea, what was funny was that it was about a stay-at-home mom and her husband and kids and the difficulties of being a stay-at-home mom versus the working mother. At a point, I indicated that the character was a white woman, and they were shocked. It never occurred to them that she wasn't black. They painted that picture in their head, and the landscape and the world that I was laying out, it was a very white world. It was clear in my mind the whole time, but it just never occurred to them that she wasn't black. So even as they're listening, I'm thinking, "Okay, the whole time, you've been sitting here thinking, 'Who's the black girl? Are people going to buy it, does this feel right, is this a little bit too outside the bounds of where people think black people exist?'" That's a weird thing. The industry has a weird relationship with black people. They like us in the past. They loved black people 30 years ago. That's great. To be a contemporary black person living in society now is kind of like weird, and that's what Shonda has been really great at. It's like these are black people from right now. They're just in there with some other white people, doing stuff. It happens.

WHAT FRUSTRATES YOU SPECIFICALLY?

Well, here's the upside and the downside, specifically of being a black writer of some intellect. I like good stuff. I've read classics. I've watched classic film, I've read classic books. I like to be smart. You can't be too smart for your audience, like you can't think that you're intellectual to the point that you lose a connection with this giant demographic that's sitting there wanting to like you. Do I want to get the black audience? Absolutely, but I'd just like a shot at the audience too. If what I come up with would just work for the audience en masse and not just for that section called "the black audience," I'd like just as much of an opportunity to do that, because no white guy is stopped from writing a script if only black people might like it. Matter of fact, that's a win. If you're a white guy and you can write some stuff that black people like, that's fantastic. Now they don't have to deal with black people. "This is great. We can get the audience, but we won't have to talk to somebody we don't understand." Then as a black writer, that feels like sort of an offense. You're like, "Well, how come I can't write for the black person? And I want to write for the white people too. I'm a guy, can I write for the women?" The women are going, "Can I write for a guy?" Can we all just do this thing? Can we all just exercise our craft? Can we all just appeal to who we appeal to? Well, no, because the people who are making decisions don't understand the dynamics of all of that. They don't know about you and your stupid art.

CHAPTER FOUR

THE POLITICS OF MAKING TELEVISION

IDEAS VS. INCOME

I n a perfect creative world, a creator/showrunner guiding their television show would never have to worry about the outside forces distracting them from the creative process of telling their story. But this is the real world, and every part of the television process is some push and pull of creative versus commerce.

However, with the expanded landscape of networks and services offering original scripted programming, a perception has evolved that there's less creative strife depending on where your show airs. In the broadcast network world, there's an entrenched idea (born out of years of war stories passed around officially and unofficially) that a showrunner's vision is rarely left alone because of nervous network and programming executives looking out for their financial investment. Meanwhile, the basic cable environment gets a much better rep because of usually shorter season orders (however, you deal with far smaller budgets). And floating on a proverbial cloud with dappled lighting, and maybe some angelic harps playing in the distance, is the world of premium cable, and, recently, streaming content development, with its storied nirvana model that promises showrunners won't get bothered at all by advertiser demands, standards and practices, or any critical feedback.

In reality, the truth lies somewhere in the murky middle for all three models, because the industry is changing at freakish pace to adapt to the ways shrinking audiences consume their television entertainment. Broadcast is greenlighting more 13-episode seasons, which used to strictly be the M.O. for basic and premium cable. There's been plenty of rumbling in the trades about problem development and "tinkering" of shows on premium cable, while basic cable programs, no matter the success, have had plenty of public budget problems that seem implausible considering the ratings earned.

"It used to be that you could understand the television universe as a solar system, and the sun was broadcast television: the three or four networks," showrunner Jeff Melvoin explains. "Everything else was a satellite that traveled around the sun, and that clearly no longer is the model. The sun has exploded, and there are a lot of little solar systems being set up, and the idea that we'll ever have a coherent whole like that again, I'm not sure we will, which is very exciting for writer/creators because the possibility will exist as we move further into the future that you can create something, and take less up front, and have more participation on the back end and have more transparency.

"One of the added skills now that you need to have to succeed as a showrunner is the ability to surf these waves," he continues, "and find where you're most comfortable, and recognize that your last ride might not match your next ride. It's all contextual. Am I doing a broadcast show? Am I doing a cable show? Am I doing an Internet show? Am I doing an international show? There's all sorts of new models creeping up where people are doing 13 episodes without a distributor. They're getting these international co-productions and then hoping that they can sell it simultaneously around the world. It's all very exciting."

Does that mean showrunners really don't have a preference about where their shows get developed or picked up? Or are the perceptions of the best places to work already out of date? Maybe it really is more of a level playing field now than ever before.

TOP: Joss Whedon; CENTER LEFT: Hart Hanson; CENTRE RIGHT: Andrew Marlowe;
BOTTOM: James Duff.

TOP LEFT: Ali LeRoi; TOP RIGHT: Kurt Sutter; CENTER LEFT: Matthew Carnahan;
CENTER RIGHT: Mike Royce; BOTTOM LEFT: Ronald D.Moore; BOTTOM RIGHT: Jeff Melvoin.

TOP LEFT: Robert and Michelle King; TOP RIGHT: Janet Tamaro; CENTER LEFT: Dee Johnson; CENTER RIGHT: Shawn Ryan; BOTTOM LEFT: John Rogers and Chris Downey; BOTTOM RIGHT: Jonathan Nolan and Greg Plageman.

TOP LEFT: Damon Lindelof ; TOP RIGHT: David Shore; CENTER LEFT: Jane Espenson; CENTER RIGHT: Bill Prady; BOTTOM LEFT: Mike Kelley; BOTTOM RIGHT: Terence Winter.

TOP LEFT: Steven S.Deknight; TOP RIGHT: J. H. Wyman.

ABOVE: Filming with James Duff in The Closer writer's room.

Filming the interview with Robert and Michelle King, showrunners on *The Good Wife*.

In conversation with David Shore on the set of *House*.

Hart Hanson making notes in the *Bones* writers' room.

Jonathan Nolan advises in the *Person of Interest* writers' room.

The Showrunners New York Comic Con panel 2013 from l-r Ryan Patrick McGuffey, Terence Winter, Ronald D.Moore, Tara Bennett, Greg Plageman, Des Doyle

The Showrunners San Diego Comic Con panel 2013 from l-r Bill Prady, Jane Espenson, Hart Hanson, Des Doyle (Director, *Showrunners*), Ryan Patrick McGuffey (Co-Producer).

THE PERCEPTION OF BROADCAST VS. CABLE

JANE ESPENSON, SHOWRUNNER: CAPRICA, HUSBANDS

Networks generally have more money to give you to produce the show, but they are broadcasters, and the word "broad" is very important, as in it has to have this broad appeal. It can't be a niche show. Cable: maybe a little less money to work with, but you can be a little more focused in your approach. You know how much more fun it is to tell a 10 percent joke than one that everybody's going to get? One that everybody's going to get is like a "knock-knock" joke. The joke that's tailored for a specific audience is a sophisticated joke and that's where cable is.

JANET TAMARO, SHOWRUNNER: RIZZOLI AND ISLES

The difference between a cable show and a network show is fewer voices weigh in on creative decisions in cable. It's the difference between trying to pick a restaurant when there are fifteen of you versus when there are four. Try it. Ask fifteen friends. "I like Ethiopian." "I like Italian." "I like Thai." Before you know it, you're eating at a diner because that's the only way to "sort of" please everyone.

I think shows can go off the rails when the head writer gets so much input and so many notes and so much criticism by a committee, that he or she begins to second guess everything. No one can create and write well in that atmosphere. You do not want to start second guessing every single creative choice. Then you're paralyzed. I have seen that happen in network more often than in cable.

JONATHAN NOLAN, SHOWRUNNER: PERSON OF INTEREST

I'm still, honestly, a big believer in broadcast. I spent the last 12 years working on film, and concentrating on the collective audience experience. TV's a little different. You watch by yourself, or with your loved ones at home. It doesn't have that collective experience, but the timing of it, the way that everyone's watching it the same night, the same hour, that experience, I think is actually really cool. I think something gets a little lost with the way that people these days consume these serialized shows all in one go. There's something really fun about watching our audience watch the show. We go out at 6pm East coast from here and watch the reactions coming in off Twitter, or online, and then you see it spread across the country. That's something really cool, and that's definitely an old-fashioned idea, but it's a cool one. It's just a different way of doing it. You still have a massive, massive audience watching broadcast television, far bigger than cable. We regularly have 14 to 15 million people watching our show, which dwarfs any of the audiences of these cable shows, but you feel like there's a way in which you can get at the quality and that long-form storytelling on broadcast. I'm excited to see where all of its going, because I think broadcast's going to head in that direction as well.

JAMES DUFF, SHOWRUNNER: THE CLOSER, MAJOR CRIMES

I hear a lot of people say things like, "I was burned by the network experience and so I went to cable," but that wasn't exactly what happened to me. Truthfully, ABC at that time was in flux and they didn't have a marketing strategy, but it wasn't like they were evil or horrible. They weren't any of those things, and that's not been my experience with networks or with studios in general. But I will say TNT has been the best place I've ever worked, and that they give me a lot of creative freedom. They give me parameters. There are rules. If you do have a negligent network president who insists on crazy things, those crazy things will become part of the forum and they will appear on television. We don't have that issue. You're going to hear a lot, I'm sure, about creative freedom and where more creative freedom rests. It's true, I think cable offers more creative freedom than network television, but they have a smaller niche to fill. If you can hit their target, which is a lot easier to hit, that's all they really care about. Networks need a broader audience and they have to take in broader considerations to get that.

DEE JOHNSON, Showrunner: Boss, Nashville

There's more creative support in the cable space than there is in the broadcast space, which (at the risk of alienating my broadcast executive friends) have reached micromanaging levels that are off the charts. I think cable feels a little less so and therefore much more attractive to creative pursuits. I think the micromanaging is, across the board, less. I mean, it's not that they're isn't the same level of care, but there's probably more of a willingness to let creative people do what creative people do, and being a little bit less beholden to the numbers of it all. It's really hard to write anything if you're thinking in your head about a dial test. It just instantly kills any sort of creativity. Those are the most painful things, I think, about getting a new show on the air, going to those focus groups and watching a dial test. Horrible.

CHRIS DOWNEY, Showrunner: Leverage

We've all been struggling. We've talked with other cable showrunners and everyone has been struggling with how to make it work. How to make a cohesive half-season that has a beginning, middle, and end, and then start another season in the winter. It's a struggle because you want to develop some continuity and some momentum. We've struggled a little bit with the ratings; they have definitely taken a hit in the winter season. It's just by virtue of the fact that people develop a habit of watching their show in the summer and they think of it as a summer show. The flip side is with so many choices for people to watch, you know that if the show is not on the air for a year, your fans could have developed a following for another show.

JOHN ROGERS, Showrunner: Leverage, The Librarians

The budget starts restrictive on a cable show. Especially since, as I've noted, that we don't have a studio. We're an independently produced television show. You make the show that you can make with the money you have. You try to stretch the dollars and you find ways that you can go cheap here to get production value over there. The budget is also restrictive on network television. It's just that at some point somebody will go and ask someone else for a lot of money, and odds are someone else will write that check. Average budgets on network television shows just run about 30 percent higher than your bog standard cable show. We're even pretty low for a cable show, to tell you the truth. Nothing extraordinarily low, but not for what you get on screen.

HART HANSON, Showrunner: Bones, The Finder, Backstrom

I think cable has an unfair advantage in absolutely every sense. The subject matter, the number of watchers that they need to stay on the air, the time they have to make their shows, the money they have to make their shows. I think it's a miracle that network television is still viable and pulling in millions and millions and millions of viewers, and I have no explanation for that. I mean, for example, Shawn Ryan: great showrunner, great writer, tried to do *Chicago Code*, a greedy cop show, on network. I thought, "Oh, he's doomed," because why wouldn't you go watch that on cable where it can actually be greedy, instead of just appearing to be greedy on network? Figuring out what a network hit is these days is pretty hard. I'm dying to go work on cable like everyone else, I think just for the time, subject matter, and seriousness you can get away with because you don't need 10 million viewers. I would be like, "Oh, heaven!"

SHAWN RYAN, Showrunner: The Shield, The Unit

I personally don't see as big a difference between network and cable as other people have. I also think that some of these cable channels have kind of perpetuated this myth that artists have complete freedom at these networks, and yet I've talked to people and heard about notes calls at these networks. So I'm not sure that's exactly it. I think it's a case-by-case situation. Does the network trust you to do the job? If they do, you're gonna get a lot of freedom. If they sense a void in leadership they're gonna rush in to fill it, no matter what network it's at.

THE 10/90 MODEL: WAVE OF THE FUTURE?

In an attempt to bypass the long-standing model of seasonal pick-ups, which means a show has a long, uncertain slog to a potential production of 100 episodes, Debmar-Mercury introduced a new production/syndication model for basic cable which packaged sitcoms in a 10/90 deal. In this arrangement, the show would get ten episodes to hit and maintain a pre-determined ratings threshold. If it does, then the series gets picked up for another 90 episodes ensuring enough programming to sell into off-network syndication stripping (or repeats). Creatively, it means a showrunner can arc out an entire lifespan of a show in a two-year span without fear of getting cancelled. It also means tighter budgets and shooting three shows a week. FX, OWN, and TBS have all tested this model with shows like *Anger Management*, *Saint George*, and *Are We There Yet?*, which was run by Ali LeRoi, who talks about the creative positives of the venture.

Ali LeRoi

❝ There was a time when a show could get through a whole season of episodes before they made a decision about it. Now, they treat television like the movies. You put two episodes out and the numbers aren't there and you're done. To know that we're doing 90, no matter what... it really is incredibly creative. It's the antithesis of what the standard network television model is because now you really are in control of your own destiny. If it's funny and you believe in it, you do it, and then you submit it to the audience and you just hope that that works. And if it doesn't then it's your fault.

When you compare these two models, the standard 20-episode order versus doing 90, if I had to pick, I'd pick the 90. It's not just that there is a degree of creative control that you have to have in order to get it done. What takes a single episode of network television comedy so long to get produced is the meetings. There's *lots* of meetings. You write an idea. You have to send it to the studio. The studio sends you back notes. You have to execute the notes. You send it back to the studio. They agree on it. Then you send it to the network. Then the network has notes. You have to execute the notes. Now, you have to send it to the studio again, make sure they're applying these notes to network again. Now, they're applying those now. Now that we all agree on what the idea is, can we put it into a beat sheet? It takes a month just to get them to sign up off on what's going to be written. Well, when you're working on your own scheduling and you've got 90 episodes, guess what? In a month, I can have nine scripts. **"**

Is Premium the Gold Standard?

When people throw around the word "cable," it can mean one of two options: basic cable, which are the upper-tier, digital package networks like SyFy, Lifetime and TNT, or premium cable, which are the subscription-based networks that cost extra every month, including HBO, Showtime, Cinemax, and Starz. In the 1990s HBO changed their own brand by investing in their scripted programming and made it prestige viewing with series like *Oz*, *The Sopranos*, and *Sex and the City*. Showtime followed with their own hits like *Dexter*, *Weeds*, and more recently *Homeland*. Even Starz got into the game and had their biggest original programming success with *Spartacus*. With unfettered censorship issues, short season models, and high production budgets, premium cable has become the coveted development ground for many showrunners because of the lure of artistic freedom, yet it does have its own sacrifices.

STEVEN S. DeKNIGHT, SHOWRUNNER: SPARTACUS

I love premium cable. I love HBO. I love Showtime. If I have one concern about it these days, it's that it's almost become a bit too self-important, to the point where it starts to feel more like homework than actually enjoying what you're watching. Some of these shows that I adore, I think they're beautifully made and just sumptuously designed and directed and written and performed, but they move at a very stately pace. What we really wanted to do with *Spartacus* is kind of what they say in *The Princess Bride*: cut out all the boring parts, and really give that kind of old-style entertainment with a new twist.

We have an incredible amount of freedom on premium cable, so going back to network television would be difficult on a creative level. Now, the trade-off, of course, is that doing 13 episodes on premium cable is not the same financial reward as doing 22 episodes on a network. I think Rob Zombie once said that "creative freedom comes with a pay cut," and he's absolutely correct. The amount of money that you can make on 22 episodes of a show in network is phenomenally large, much larger than I make on this show.

I have ideas and concepts that would work better on a network show than on premium cable, but I do have that taste of that freedom. And to be able to have a conversation where two people can talk the way two people would talk without artificial constraints was just amazingly liberating. It's as simple a thing as it is to have somebody be able to say "fuck," which I hear in my daily life 20, 30 times a day. Also, I'm from New Jersey, so I tend to use it a lot, and that kind of natural rhythm to dialogue in speech is invaluable. Not to mention the fact that you can have two people who are romantically involved, and you can take it to a level that is natural, and you don't have to worry about when you're shooting saying I've got to make sure there's no nipple, or I know that the studio and network will only allow me, like, 10 percent side boob. Not to have to worry about that stuff is incredible.

TERENCE WINTER, Showrunner: Boardwalk Empire

There is a great deal of creative freedom, and that's one of the great things about working for HBO. I think they hire people whom they respect, and they let you do your job. It's not to say there aren't conversations. There are, but there are never mandates, and there are never notes that are born of cowardice where they're afraid to alienate people or offend people. They're not trying to sell commercial airtime or products. It's based on, "just do the best show you can do."

Creatively, we've been able to do everything we've ever wanted. With that freedom, it's almost like Spider-Man: with great power comes great responsibility. That's true in television too. I don't do things that are over-the-top just because we might be able to get away with them. As graphic as the show can be in terms of violence or the types of storytelling we do, we don't push the envelope gratuitously.

On broadcast TV, it would be a vastly different show. Not even from the standpoint of violence and nudity, I just think the manner of storytelling is just alien to network shows. I'm assuming that people watching my show are very,

very bright. They're interested in history and they are willing to stay with the show and pay attention. I don't know if that's the case for a lot of network shows. I'm not just trying to take a swipe at network shows. I think they're in a different business, and I just don't think this fits the model of what they're trying to do. I think if you try to say, "Oh, I'm going to go to a network, and I'm going to do a show like we do on cable," you're setting yourself up for a therapist's office, because it's just not going to happen. Despite the times that the networks have said they do want to try to do more edgy material, or more thought-provoking material, it just doesn't ever really seem to get there.

Off the Radar Shows

With the tremendous amount of original programming available now—both scripted and reality—getting a show to rise above the din to get traction with television critics, audiences, and/or social media is incredibly important for ratings and longevity. But if a show doesn't get the same buzz as a *Game of Thrones*, *Mad Men*, or *Breaking Bad*, does that mean it's not good? Of course not, but for some shows it can certainly put them in a disappointing "red-headed stepchild" position that can be frustrating to overcome. *Army Wives* showrunner Jeff Melvoin talks about how the series battled that problem.

Jeff Melvoin
❝ Lifetime was great. It's not a question of that they didn't support it or put money behind the promotion of it, I just think that perception is so important. If people think that Lifetime's a certain category, they're not going to give it the critical

respect that they would another show. And, if it's called *Army Wives*, I think a lot of people like me, thought, 'Oh, it's in the same category as *Desperate Housewives*,' which means it's not to be taken seriously. I'm not bitter about it. I just think it's a fact.

'Let's just compare that *Mad Men*, another terrific show, had a high rating, and it was 3.5 million people. *Army Wives*' highest rated show was 4.8 million people. Routinely, our numbers were significantly higher than that. I'm not comparing the two shows in any critical way. There's a report called 'The Stickiness Factor' which shows how loyal viewers are, and two years in a row *Army Wives* was the number one basic cable show in terms of stickiness. If viewers like our show, they stick with the show. But people don't get points in the Hamptons in August talking about *Army Wives*. Our audience was fiercely loyal and loved the show. But those are the breaks. I believe that the show probably would have a wider critical following and more buzz if it was on a different network, and had a different launch somehow. It is an odd state of affairs these days in terms of prestige versus actual numbers versus revenues, which are very highly protected depending on who the network is. I think it's fascinating. **"**

THE DREADED NETWORK NOTES

Perhaps one of the most soul-killing and tedious creative hurdles a showrunner has to traverse is what the industry calls a "notes session," or a "notes call," with the network executives and studio executives. A bad note can ignite epic creative firestorms, or even ruin creative partnerships. It's that sensitive place where the creative often bristle at the perception of the "suits" arbitrarily picking apart their hard work.

Here's how it works: the showrunner on a series for every episode has to submit outlines, and then scripts, for the network and studio to review. Why? Because the networks and studios pay for the show to be produced, so it's within their rights, and best interest, to review every line that is going to get produced and eventually air. Where problems start to flare is when executives don't see eye-to-eye with the creative vision of a showrunner. Or perhaps they don't understand, or trust, the nuance or direction the story or character is going. This is when the executives will provide their "notes" and recommendations, or even demands, for changes.

The best-case scenario is that a showrunner will accept the note, or the intention of the note, and make a clarification change, or compromise, that might make the script even better. The worst case scenario is receiving random, strange, or just plain bad suggestions about the script that seem impossible to accomplish without some tremendous creative compromise, or just selling out, by the showrunner and his writing team. Learning how to deal with difficult notes is one of the skills a showrunner has to master to service not only their show but their financier overlords. So what is the prevalent general consensus from showrunners about the notes process? Do they look at it as a positive, or as a migraine in the making?

MIKE KELLEY, SHOWRUNNER: REVENGE

Notes, when they're given in the best of circumstances, help elevate the material. The time when notes suck and injure you is when they're given out of fear. Unfortunately, fear is something that seems to permeate the halls of all networks and studios and writers' offices, too. If you're in the creative business, a healthy dose of fear is what you can expect.

JANE ESPENSON, Showrunner: Caprica, Husbands

Notes can be very, very useful. When the studio and the network work best is when they are functioning as a very well-informed viewer. They have a little more objectivity and distance than you do, so they can say, "The audience is going to notice that this is actually a repeat of the information in the earlier scene." Or, "The audience may be confused here, because they could well think that they're supposed to be drawing this inference." Or, "The audience might be bored here, because you realize that the scene has gone on a bit long." They're fantastic at making sure that the story you're telling is the story you think you're telling.

HART HANSON, Showrunner: Bones, The Finder, Backstrom

I get some really good notes from these people. Usually not the ones I'm expecting. Out of left field, our network or studio executive will say, "You should do B," and I go, "Oh my God. That's so true." When you disagree with them it's not like, "These people are so stupid." Unfortunately, they are so smart. If they could do the typing they would do it themselves but they're very smart people and they have an agenda.

ALI LeROI, Showrunner: Everybody Hates Chris, Are We There Yet?

Chris [Rock] and I used to have this conversation and we'd go, "Ignore the note, but respect the reaction." You know if somebody is reading your bit and they go "Hmmmm," it doesn't mean that what you've come up with is something bad. It just means that you didn't necessarily convey it in a way that they get it, and you have to do that. People need to get it if you want them to be entertained.

DAVID SHORE, SHOWRUNNER: HOUSE

I have very little sympathy for showrunners who just ignore notes. [The notes] are sometimes stupid but if somebody's not reacting to something, it means you didn't do something right. The person reading your script is your audience and you have to listen to them, even if they're working in a big tower and wear a suit. I also recognize I don't own this show. They own the show. I'm doing a job. I have to respect that. The freedom they give me, and I will keep fighting for more and more freedom, it's a gift. It's not even a gift, I'm actually charging for it, so I mean it's even better than a gift.

JONATHAN NOLAN, SHOWRUNNER: PERSON OF INTEREST

I'd heard all these horror stories about network shows, and how if things aren't going the right way, they dig in with the notes. [Greg] and I probably handled something in the region of 300 to 400 notes calls. On *The Dark Knight* I had none of those calls, so this is a real change of pace for me. But I think that's because we approached it with, hopefully, a confident, clear, unified voice. If we had any disagreements, I don't think anyone knows about them because we had them privately. Largely we saw eye-to-eye on everything, and then presented all that with a unified voice to the studio and the network, and they were fucking relieved, because that's really all they want. They just want someone who has a vision for something that's maybe a little risky, a little different from what they're doing, but not a million miles outside of it.

NOTES MEETING 101

While every studio and network regime has their own way of dispensing notes, the process is relatively cut and dry. Jane Espenson explains the ins and outs.

Jane Espenson

❝ Different networks and studios structure their corporate executive ranks differently. You may be dealing with someone who gives notes only on new shows, versus someone who gives notes on continuing shows. Or you may have different layers of executives weighing in, so you have to know that a senior person's notes supersede the less senior person's notes. Each place seems to do it a little differently.

"The showrunner can either be alone on the notes call with the network and studio, which may be one notes call, or it may be two separate notes calls. Or they may bring the [episode] writer in with them to get their notes personally. It just depends on how it's done. The showrunner may come back and relay, 'Here are the notes that I got from the studio.' It may come in an email. The individual writer should be very clear after a notes session. The showrunner should be very clear with them about which notes they're expected to address, and which ones they're not expected to address.

"Ron Moore at *Battlestar Galactica* had a very good system. He would get the notes email, he would then go through it and send an email to you, forward those notes to you, but he would notate after each note, 'We agreed to do this one; I don't think this one's worth doing. Do you have a suggestion for that?' You would see everything that the studio said, unambiguously, because they were forced to write it all out, and you would see what Ron wanted you to do with it. It's a great system. I liked it, because it forced the network to be very specific in their notes, and the writer had a written thing they could go back and consult. Did I address this note? Yes. Check it off. **"**

Stuck in the Middle

Unfortunately, showrunners can get squeezed in a notes session because of the politics going on between their financiers—the network and the studio. Those two entities can sometimes be working under the same corporate entity, like when an ABC Studios-produced series airs on ABC. But you can also have a studio, like Warner Bros, producing a series that is aired on FOX. "There's a huge division between [networks and studios]," showrunner Hart Hanson of *Bones* explains. "Everybody has a different agenda, and I don't mean that in a cruel way. They have different business models. The networks want the American viewers. The studio wants something that will perform on DVD, DVR, and foreign sales. They have different ideas of what the show should be, which differ from the network."

This means that if the two companies aren't agreeing on licensing fees, off-net intentions, or something as petty as executives across companies just not liking each other, it puts the showrunner in a bad spot. The showrunner may have to suffer quietly, or try to navigate the battlefield when the notes they receive are really about everything but the actual script at hand.

JOHN ROGERS, Showrunner: Leverage, The Librarians

Studios can own networks. Where you would think that would make it easier, actually the turf wars between the two parts of the company become really vicious. You start, as a writer/creator, getting caught in the power struggles of those executives. That's pretty nasty and pretty ugly. Writers tend to be the fodder that gets fed into that. The script becomes the battleground, and the only casualty is the person that typed it as opposed to the suits.

PICK YOUR BATTLES

What if a note is really atrocious? Is it a showrunner's duty to then fight a note if it could hurt a show? Or is diplomacy always the better route?

JOHN ROGERS

Two of our writers actually named their company "This is the Hill Productions," because the thing we beat into the young writers when they start is, "This the hill that you're going to die on." This note, this moment, this script, this argument you have is the only one you're ever going to have a shot at winning, so, make sure it's the one. After that, if you just start fighting them on every single thing, you become the problem in the room. They write the checks and they pay the bills, and, by the way, sometimes there's no way to get out of it.

HART HANSON, Showrunner: Bones, The Finder, Backstrom

You pick your hill to die on, so it better be worth it. In the first season of *Bones*, we were arguing about casting one particular episode—and I'll never do this again—but I said to the network casting people, "Fine. You cast this episode. Go ahead. You know so much. You cast this episode," and it sucked. They did not know how to cast this episode, but nor should they have known. I had no right to say, "Fine. You cast it." They are not the doers; they are the commenters. They are the people who say, "I don't like this actor for this reason." I just got tired and angry and abdicated my job, which I will never do again. I don't even blame them, and it's no kind of victory that there's this bad episode there. I'm the one who's supposed to know what actors I need, the tone, the field, the phase, the mix. That's my job, not their job.

ALI LeROI , Showrunner: Everybody Hates Chris, Are We There Yet?

The tough thing about getting the crazy note is you don't need to overreact. The reality of the process is that if you just stay calm, and acknowledge the fact that there is something that needs to be addressed, chances are, because this suite of executives is so busy troubleshooting the real problems, if it's something minor they're probably going to forget it, or you're going to go shoot it and if your idea works, fine. If it doesn't, whatever, it's not going to be the end of the world. So if you make a big deal out of protesting something minor, then you're just drawing everybody's attention to it. Now you're in a clusterfuck, and who wants to be in that?

HART HANSON

I know enough to embrace the idea that if the network gives us a note saying, "We really don't like this," I'll say, "Let's do a reshoot!" So I'll give part of what they want and *lots* of what I want to fix it. Now they're finding it expensive to give me notes, which is genius. I wish I'd thought of it before. I'm delighted they're paying for it. I was trained in Canada where you didn't have that kind of money. (*Laughs*)

ALI LEROI

The dumbest note, the single dumbest note I've ever gotten was when we were doing *Everybody Hates Chris* and we had an episode where Chris had gotten a fever or flu or something. It was a Christmas Eve. He was in the hospital and he was hallucinating that he was talking to a guy, who was basically Santa Claus. He's an old guy laying on a bed spouting off philosophy about who deserves to be given this and "what type of life do you have?" All this type of stuff. We were looking at a John Goodman type or something like that, and the note came down from the network, "Does Santa Claus have to be so old?"

HART HANSON

The worst point for notes is before you're on the air and everybody thinks they know how the public is going to react to a show, how the audience is going to react, or if a show is doing kind of middling well, which is what *Bones* did. It did middling well. It was not a hit. The notes during the time that we were a middling success, there were lots of them. How do we make the show? How do we do better? I would always say, "More promotion would help. Put us in one time slot." They'd say, "No, what if it was more procedural?"

IN DEPTH:

ORIGINAL VOICES IN CABLE

One of the loudest showrunner proponents for the creative positives of the basic cable network landscape is Kurt Sutter. An executive producer on *The Shield*, Sutter followed that series up with his own creation, *Sons of Anarchy*, which is a loosely based *Hamlet* on Harleys. In its seven seasons on FX, *Sons* pushed boundaries by graphically portraying violence and exposing the dark underbelly of drugs and gun-running in the MC culture. It found its audience and steadily gained viewership every season, making it one of FX's biggest hits ever. Sutter advocates that cable is truly the bastion of original storytelling in television, cultivating outside-the-box ideas with creative budgeting that ensures profits.

KURT SUTTER

Look, I think if you have an original voice, and you're able to put that on paper, then I do believe that there's a lot of smart people in this town that will recognize that and will create that and speak to that. There's a culture, I think especially on broadcast television, that it's sort of a joke, the idea that, "This season we're going to do something completely new and we want completely new and original ideas."

At the end of the day, what they want is the same old shit. It's why you find, when you have a show that does well, suddenly you will have a dozen clones, and as a result of that there's a stifling of creativity, there's a stifling of originality, and that you have writers that don't try to come up with original things. They try to come up with things that they think perhaps will sell. So, it's not just the burden on the creator, I think it's a burden on the whole industry to a certain extent that it's not an industry right now in a lot of areas, in terms of broadcast, that really fosters and encourages anything that's remotely groundbreaking.

That's why I think most of the original voices are attracted to cable or to pay. First of all, you have a much bigger scope in terms of budget, so you can go to an HBO that has a deal with the BBC and say, "Hey, what about?" And you have the resources and the talent to make that happen. But on a smaller scale you can go, "Hey, I have an idea about a show that takes place in the world of outlaw bikers." You wouldn't be able to sell that pitch anywhere else.

The same way pitching a show about outlaw bikers would be a very difficult sell to Fox proper, but it's an easier show and an interesting sell to someone like FX or AMC, or some of the other networks that are now venturing into original programming.

I know myself well enough as an artist to know that chances are I'm never really going to do a network show, just because of my sensibilities as a writer and the things I gravitate towards. Knowing my personality, in terms of having a lot of hands stirring the soup, I don't do well with that. But the truth is I never had that experience. I've never really done a show on a network so I'm kind of speaking out of my ass to a certain extent in that I've never done that. But I think I can take a step back and look at the landscape of what shows are on the air and speak to my colleagues and really understand why, season after season, only every once in a while do you have a show that breaks the mould and is doing something original like *Lost* or unfortunately shows like Fox's *Lone Star*. That was an original idea and it went away because the audience did not show up in time.

I do have a show that, on one level, critics understand and can appreciate and can applaud, but the same time I have a show that's big and exciting that I think appeals to a much more broad audience than *Breaking Bad* would, or even on our own network, *Justified*, which is a brilliant show. But I think because it's a more subtle show, it doesn't reach the scope of the audience that we have. I bring that up because the audience is incredibly committed to the show to the point where it frightens me sometimes. They feel like they own the show; they feel like they're part of the show. They can associate with the world and they feel that we give a shit. I think in general that's what happens in cable, that you're allowed to tell these stories in a much more complex way. They're subtle, the characters are much better defined, and perhaps the stories unfold a little slower than they would on network.

For the most part you can have a show that does numbers that would be minuscule compared to broadcast standards, but be enough to sustain the advertising revenue needed to generate the episodes of the show and therefore, you know, on *The Shield*, we had a few bells and whistles as the series progressed and brought on Glenn Close and Forest Whitaker. We would see spikes in terms of ratings, but for the most part we had that solid 2.5 million that were die-hard fans that showed up every week, and yes, we did much more on DVD and ultimately towards the end when TiVo was involved we did more on DVR. But that solid core tuning in—people that showed up week in, week out—that was enough to really keep that engine running, and that allowed us to play up the model, which kind of runs out after about seven seasons.

CHAPTER FIVE

THE SHOWRUNNER AS PRODUCER

SHOWRUN-YIN AND YANG

Former *Buffy The Vampire Slayer* showrunner Joss Whedon opines, "Being a showrunner is utterly consuming. You're editing and writing and directing and doing 100 different things at once. It's draining. It's awful. I miss it terribly because it is also feeding you at the same time as it's taking away from you. It's a constant outflow and you're seeing responses and you're having this dialog with an audience that you don't have in any other way."

Joss Whedon's love/hate relationship with the gig is one shared by many of his colleagues who get the rare opportunity to run their own series. When talking about the job, there's a consistent tone of exhaustion that underscores everything the showrunners discuss, but there's also a light in their eyes that helps explain the push and pull of the position. Showrunning gives a storyteller incredible access to the money, actors, and talented below-the-line crew members who will bring their mind's vision to life onscreen. It's an incredible position to be in, but there's always a cost.

The hours, the impact on their families, the delicate creative management of the people who work for them, and the eventual burnout are real factors that come with the job, but aren't often addressed publicly. There are many reasons for this, the biggest arguably being that showrunners don't want to run the risk of sounding whiny or ungrateful when they're afforded such an exceptional opportunity. They also don't have much time to talk about the downsides when they're overwhelmed actually doing the job, or trying to eke out whatever free time they can with their loved ones. But if showrunning is a goal for any writer coming up through the ranks, the darker stuff to traverse is as important to know, and prepare for, as the fun stuff.

The Worst Parts of Showrunning

JOSS WHEDON, Showrunner: Buffy the Vampire Slayer, Firefly, Dollhouse

I would say the thing I enjoy the least is probably the tonnage. It's the fact that something is always going wrong and that you never know what it's going to be. Eventually, somebody hands you a choice of props and you want to beat them over the head with them because you don't want to choose a prop. The middle of breaking a story when you have an idea for a story—it's a great feeling when you're trying to structure that story. When you're in the process of writing it, that's lovely. It's the work portion of the work that makes me a little nuts.

DAVID SHORE, Showrunner: House

Anything that's bureaucratic is just… I would have stayed a lawyer if I enjoyed that stuff. It's the creative stuff. It's the story. It's not like it's fun while I'm actually doing it, but every now and again I have a moment while we're doing it, or after I'm doing it, where I kind of go, "That was good. That was pretty good. That was pretty clever," and I feel good about that.

RONALD D. MOORE, Showrunner: Battlestar Galactica, Outlander

I think the parts of the job I don't enjoy are the political parts of the job; trying to navigate the politics of a studio and a network at the same time is difficult.

SHAWN RYAN, Showrunner: The Shield, The Unit

Well, showrunners, we feel sorry for ourselves a lot so it's easy for us to say it's the hardest job in show business. I'm sure that somebody who was a network president might think they have the toughest job. I actually think being a crew member is the toughest job in Hollywood. You know, I don't get to go to set a lot but I'm there for my pilots and I'm always amazed at what the crews do and the hours they work. So I would not say it's the toughest job, but it is a high-wire act and it's easy to fall, and it's easy to fail.

TERENCE WINTER, SHOWRUNNER: BOARDWALK EMPIRE

It's difficult for everybody. I think it's more difficult on the people who work on the crew. They're on the set every day, 15 hours a day, five days a week. I can't run a writers' room for 15 hours straight or our heads would explode. I do get to go home and see my kids and occasionally put them to bed. I get up early so I can see them in the morning. I think a lot of people who say they want to be in show business don't really know what they're asking for. It sounds glamorous but it's really hard work; it's grueling and very long hours. Chances are you will not see a lot of your family if you're in this business.

DEE JOHNSON, SHOWRUNNER: BOSS, NASHVILLE

Surviving the soul murder part of it. I think on the surface of it, [the job] probably looks a lot of fun. Any job, creatively—particularly in television—you have to be able to deal with perhaps 95 percent of it being your ability to withstand criticism of one sort or another and either rebound from it or improve from it. I think it's really challenging and it's not set up to necessarily bolster your ego. I think that's probably the hardest part about it.

JONATHAN NOLAN, SHOWRUNNER: PERSON OF INTEREST

My wife is a TV writer and producer and I keep saying, "You didn't warn me. You didn't tell me!" I kind of knew. I'd seen it through my wife's eyes. If I had any illusions, Greg [Plageman] very quickly disillusioned me when we first sat down. It's a wild, wooly, crazy job, but it's been a fun one. It does tend to take over your entire life, and I don't think I'd necessarily anticipated that.

HART HANSON, SHOWRUNNER: BONES, THE FINDER, BACKSTROM

It's more just by the end of the day… everyone's pecking at you. I do think that one of the downsides of being a showrunner is that if you're doing it correctly, everyone that you come into contact with is just a little annoyed with you. Something about your interaction is annoying them: actors, the other writers, the other producers, the network, the studio.

JANET TAMARO, Showrunner: Rizzoli & Isles

The worst part is having to triage. Every day, you have to decide, "Is this the hill I want to die on?" How many of these critical details can I live without? There is only so much you can focus on. And the rest has to be delegated or discarded.

JAMES DUFF, Showrunner: The Closer, Major Crimes

The hardest thing about this job, aside from the hours and not seeing my friends and family the way I used to, is how much I must struggle to keep physically writing. Not editing or mixing but actually putting my fingers on the keyboard and writing the words. That's who I am. I am a writer, first and foremost, not a producer and a director. I love writing, and fighting for that time—that time to be alone with a story myself—that has been the biggest challenge I face on a day-to-day basis.

KURT SUTTER, Showrunner: Sons of Anarchy

I gladly give interviews and I gladly talk to the press, but it's the extracurricular stuff that goes along with the job sometimes that can really be draining. I gladly do it because I know it's going to service the show and help, but especially when you get towards the premier of the show, and usually at that point I'm in episode 11 or 12 crawling my way towards the finish line, where suddenly you're doing days and days of interviews, and that can be a little grueling.

JOHN ROGERS, Showrunner: Leverage, The Librarians

Our first showrunner was David Landsberg, a great 1980s showrunner who came up, and his big thing was, "My job is to take the shit and give the credit. I am the dude who protects you from the suits, the actors, everything, so that you can do good creative work, and it might need some shining that I'll put on it, but that's my gig." We both kind of internalized that so our room is not going to be the one where we fire hose our problems on the writers. That's why the executive producer is in front of our names, and not in front of other people's names, because we are supposed to bear that responsibility and get the god damned job done without making a drama out of it.

ANDREW MARLOWE, SHOWRUNNER: CASTLE

The part that I don't love is that there is a political component that goes along with it in terms of people who I've never met taking credit for the show, and just having to be patient and gracious because I know that those are the people who we are partnered with in various aspects. Navigating some of the difficult political agendas that sometimes you get in television is not the most pleasant part of the job.

The part I really hate is when we're doing staffing. I read a script by a writer and it's a good script—and I know that the writer's put a lot of time and energy into it. I know that they're probably really talented—but it's not fitting with what we're doing. Then I have to get on the phone with the agent and say, "This person just isn't right." As a writer myself, I feel that pang of what it's like to be on the other side of the phone call. That's hard for me.

BURNOUT

With a schedule of creative delivery as punishing as a typical broadcast season is, there's no doubt that burnout becomes a factor with showrunners and their writers who have been in the business over progressive shows. *The Big Bang Theory* showrunner Bill Prady admits,

❝ I think the burnout rate for showrunners is 100 percent. 100 percent of the people who do this stop in their mid to late 50s, whether in success or failure, and I think some people, you succeed, you create a show, you have enough money to retire, or you fail.

"Here's a way to think about it. I often think about Charlie Bucket [of Roald Dahl's *Willy Wonka and the Chocolate Factory*], and Charlie Bucket gets a golden ticket into Mr. Wonka's factory. He goes through on the tour and he's the only one who makes it, and at the end, Mr. Wonka says to him, 'Charlie this is yours. The factory is yours.'

"That's got to be a great day, and the next day has got to be an amazing day, and the next week when you bring your friends over and you say, 'This is my chocolate factory now. This is pretty good.' About a month in, when you're sitting down in a production meeting and you've got a couple of Oompa-Loompas there, and you say, 'Listen, we're really having a hard time. We've got a problem with the cocoa shipments that are coming in and a lot of the stuff is locked on a ship and we cannot get it through the Panama Canal so were going to have to shut down the number two assembly line.' By the time

Charlie Bucket gets there and realizes what this job actually is, he's going to be at a point where if he turns and says, 'I don't want this. I don't want the chocolate factory anymore,' people are going to go, 'Oh my God are you mad? How could you give this up?' 'But I'm exhausted.'

"That's the problem. It's too good to quit and it's too hard to do. The system, they will keep trying to make you comfortable. They will do everything they can think. of. They will give you money. They will bring you anything you want for lunch. You name it and they'll bring it to you for lunch, which is why I had to fight this year to take off 25 pounds. They will start catering to you on a level that is regal, all to keep you comfortable, all to keep you there, all to keep you doing it, all to keep you turning out the next episode because they need the next episode. If you said to them the only way I'm going to be a able to produce the next episode is on a hospital gurney with an I.V. running into my vein, they would say, 'Great, what kind of gurney do you like because here are three choices, and what would you like in the I.V.?' **"**

Long Hours? You Betcha!

JOSS WHEDON, SHOWRUNNER: BUFFY THE VAMPIRE SLAYER, FIREFLY, DOLLHOUSE

You don't go into a TV show expecting good hours. You're not expecting a happy normal life; you go into a TV show expecting the worst. You expect a campaign where you're charging through the mud for months and months and sending letters to home and it's very *G.I. Joe* (the old one, not the new one). You go in expecting the worst, but very often it is not the worst. I was first in and last out. If you're doing that I think people are more forgiving. I do remember saying one time that the first year of *Buffy* was like everybody was on ecstasy, everybody hated everybody. Everybody loved everybody. Nobody wanted to go home. That's how I described it. And my wife just quietly said, "I think the crew wanted to go home." I was like, "Oh yeah, good point."

JANET TAMARO, SHOWRUNNER: RIZZOLI & ISLES

It consumes you. Every night, every weekend. There are no vacations. It's like having colicky quintuplet newborns—who stay newborns. A production demands every bit of your energy. Something or someone is always breaking. There's a constant barrage of phone calls, email, texts, IMs, streaming, you name it. You are never NOT making a television show.

J.H. WYMAN, SHOWRUNNER: FRINGE, ALMOST HUMAN

We'll put in a lot of hours, but at the end of the day, we're not building hospitals. We're making a television show, so… any problem is surmountable. It's just relying on our staffs, relying on each other, relying on our cast and crew. The hardest thing is that the downtime is largely spent thinking about, "Oh, what are the plates spinning in the air that are about to drop?" We always talk about triage. There's always something that's an immediate issue that needs to be dealt with and then there are four issues behind it. You've all seen the famous episode of *I Love Lucy*, with the chocolates on the conveyor belt? It's very much like that. If you drop a chocolate, there's seven others that are going to fall when you try to pick it up.

BILL PRADY, Showrunner: The Big Bang Theory

The writers start working in June. We start shooting in August and we wrap in April and I think that if you would bring in scientists to study this, they would discover that human beings have exactly enough energy to accomplish 90 percent of that schedule and the last 10 percent of it is a Bataan Death March to the wrap party.

JOHN ROGERS, Showrunner: Leverage, The Librarians

There's also a certain culture of showrunner that kind of thrives on crisis and loves to blame the production for being the reason that they're there until midnight. They would just be there until midnight if even nothing was shooting. [Chris Downey and I] were both on shows where you were there until midnight. It doesn't get better after ten o'clock at night. It just doesn't, you know. Come in, do your best, do your job, be with your friends, make something good, go home, repeat.

SHAWN RYAN, Showrunner: The Shield, The Unit

The real thing that makes you weary I find is that when you're writing a show, your brain doesn't get a break. Your brain doesn't get a vacation even when you're on vacation. You're always thinking about the deadlines that are coming up. You're thinking days ahead about how you're gonna get these things done and then of course the next day some emergency happens that screws up your entire plan. So yes, the hours are really long, but really it's the brain hours that I find even worse.

JAMES DUFF, Showrunner: The Closer, Major Crimes

The principal objective in performing one's duties here is to get the work done without losing entirely your friends and your family, because it's just so many hours. In fact, I'm having a going-away party this year in June, once we start mixing, to say goodbye to my friends. I'm going to say, "Pretend I'm in Vancouver. Pretend I'm in Toronto. Don't call me for birthdays. Don't call me for christenings. Don't call me for anything but a death or a wedding." You have to let go of your life to do this job, let go of your family, let go of your friends, and filling that void with social media isn't for everybody.

ANDREW MARLOWE, Showrunner: Castle

For me, having my wife [Terri Edda Miller] on [*Castle*] is essential to the success of this particular show. There are stretches during the season where I have to work four, five, six weekends in a row, both Saturday and Sunday. Then I wake up and I haven't really been home in 45 or 50 days. Having somebody who's on the show being supportive in that relationship, being able to have a creative conversation with you about what's going on, being somebody to bounce stuff off of, and being as in the character's heads as I am, is really invaluable. Otherwise I'd feel disconnected from my life, disconnected from my creative process. So it's been great, maddening at times, but maddening in the same way that working with anybody else is maddening, but really great, really valuable.

DAMON LINDELOF, Showrunner: Lost, The Leftovers

My own personal philosophy about showrunning—and I know that Carlton shares it because we were partners—was it's a slightly monastic existence. It's all you really have time to do. I basically proposed marriage in May right after the *Lost* pilot was picked up, thinking that the show would probably be canceled after a few episodes. Then I got married three days after the season one finale when everybody went sailing off in the raft and then the raft got blown up. Then I had my son right around the time that Locke and Jack were going into the hatch. So, the fact that the benchmarks of my life are measured by the show, shouldn't it be the other way around?

DAVID SHORE, Showrunner: House

Anytime I have to deal with any other human being other than a writer tends to be a chore for me, and even with writers half the time. The effect of this on my personal life… I'm still married. My kids still claim they love me, two of the three of them do, which is pretty good at this point. It is tricky. You try and make the time. You try and keep the weekends free. It has been easier to do that the last few years. A price is paid, but a price is paid for almost any job, and now I feel like I'm rationalizing. I'm going home now. I have to go kiss my kids.

The Care and Feeding of Your Actors

I t's not a secret that many television writers are very sensitive when it comes to people tinkering with their words, be it network execs, studio execs, or actors. It might seem like a writer is being precious when they consider the scripted words sacred, and in some instances they are. But that's what writers get paid for in television: to spend a lot of time drafting and redrafting the words and language to create intent and character progression that makes the series (hopefully) increase in quality episode after episode.

It's one of the reasons why showrunners and writers aren't fond of it when actors casually talk about how much improv they do, or how they change the script for the better. A lot of writers wouldn't deign to do what their cast does in the show, so they would like the same respect in return. When that doesn't happen, it's often the spark that sets off those dramatic, behind-the-scenes fights between actors and showrunners that can sometimes cause *a lot* of strain on the production side.

Sensitive egos aside, what a showrunner strives for is a relationship with their actors where they can talk about character issues in a script and it doesn't result in a possessive screaming match. Luckily, it's very possible, but it's often down to how a showrunner sets the tone and paths of communication. Here's how some of them deal with their thespian issues.

MIKE KELLEY, SHOWRUNNER: SWINGTOWN, REVENGE

I think that these feuds that are happening between the showrunners and their actors, more often than not, seem to come out of two really creative people that have a disagreement. It builds from passion. If you're lucky, the arguments that you have with your performers are all based on character and story and trying to do the best show that you possibly can. When I'm dealing with my cast, the occasional hot temper is impossible to avoid because everybody is so exposed. You're so exposed as a writer. You're so exposed as a performer. So, insecurities and frustrations are going to bleed in. I know frustrations would mean that I'm not accessible in a lot of ways because we are separated or I'm just too buried in trying to keep the boat afloat.

Those things are going to lend themselves to some pretty fraught territory. The way I try to handle it is I try to sift through what is constructive. If there's an argument that's being had, I try to focus on what's constructive in there because, generally, there's a note to be had inside a vicious, throw-down argument that might be helpful for the show. I always try to say in the back of my head, "What's best for the show?" That's what I always tell them if somebody says they're not going to say this, which is rare. I'm one of these few people that, I think, loves getting people's thoughts. I want to know what you think. [Actors] are the custodians of the character, really. Their opinion is important to me, especially if I'm doing something that contradicts anything that they've chosen. I think that if you go out as far as asking yourself what's best for the show and try to put your ego down just a bit and try to understand that these people are under a lot of pressure, too. It's their faces out there. They're the ones getting stopped on the street.

JANET TAMARO, SHOWRUNNER: RIZZOLI & ISLES

I love working with actors. I love seeing my words on the page come to life in wonderfully surprising and unexpected ways when they trigger a performance by a talented actor. The best part about a series is you get to know your actors. You form a partnership—and start to discover who they are and the traits they bring to a character. When I first started writing scripts and was a lowly staff writer, I wrote a scene for an actor who wouldn't take off his shirt. He was really self-conscious about his gut, which means you'll end up with a self-conscious performance.

I would never force actors to do things they absolutely do not want to do. I haven't faced that situation too much. I think this show offers something that a lot of procedurals don't, which is the actors get to be funny, which all of them love. They are all naturally funny people. I try hard to write a range of stories and emotions so they get to go different places. They're not just doing low-velocity blood spatter. They're not the exposition train. I let them be people. We only go home with Jane and with Maura. I allow them to be fully realized people as best I can within the confines of the show. I've been told how refreshing and great and awesome and terrific this is from the actors: "Thank you for letting me be in a scene where I can tear up and put my head on a desk and then the next scene I get to say something that's really wildly funny." I think that has helped me not have conflicts with actors. I give them a lot to do.

ANDREW MARLOWE, SHOWRUNNER: CASTLE

[On *Castle*] Nathan [Fillion] will have opinions, Stana [Katic] will have opinions, and Jon [Huertas] and Seamus [Dever] and the other [actors] will come to me with thoughts. Usually it's on a line level. Usually it's like, "Hey, can I say this instead of that," or "Here's a great opportunity."

We understand that these guys spend all day with their characters, especially some of the secondary characters. They've explored those characters more than we might have here when we have to juggle eight or nine characters and give all of them a voice. So sometimes they come with really interesting insights and those insights are worth listening to. Other times they're not, and we have a conversation of why that's not going to help the show.

BILL PRADY, SHOWRUNNER: THE BIG BANG THEORY

Trust is earned, and what we have always shown the cast is that if something isn't working, we will see it and we will change it. We are never going to get to the point where we're standing in front of the audience filming a scene that isn't fundamentally right for these characters, both from a character point of view and especially from a comedy point of view, so you earn that trust. You earn that trust by bringing them a good script at the table-read, and when stuff doesn't work, you fix it, and the cast says, "Even if this isn't right on Thursday, I'm pretty sure it's going to be right by Friday without me saying anything."

DAVID SHORE, Showrunner: House

It's a wonderful thing for me that I have a star [Hugh Laurie] who sees the character the same way I do and is attracted to the same things about this character that I am. That doesn't mean that we always see things the exact same way, but I cannot remember ever having a fight with him about things that House would do. He comes to me with his input, his thoughts. He usually comes with three or four thoughts per episode, sometimes just a line or two. Then when he's on the set, he's thought through these scenes. When he has something to say, we pay attention, because nine times out of ten, he's right. He gets this character. He gets the show and he's thought it through. It's like having an extra director on the set as well.

HART HANSON, Showrunner: Bones, The Finder, Backstrom

There's a [Steven] Bochco quote I heard [about actors], which was "The first year, they work for you. Second year, you're partners. The third year, you work for them." The reason being is that if a show is in its third year, it's a hit. You can replace behind the camera. You cannot replace in front of the camera. If there's a huge fight, if you're not getting along, and it comes to who's going to stay, the actor will probably win.

I have a deal with actors that I will discuss any scene, anything they want to discuss in a scene, as long as it's 24 hours before we shoot it. I think it's very bad to go to the set and change a scene. For one thing, I have too many things in my head. I don't have a good enough memory to know, "Well, how is this going to affect down the line? What have we shot? What haven't we shot?" I believe that directors and actors deserve a lot of time with what they have to do with their day's work, especially the good-hearted, hard-working actors who prepare the day before. Those are valuable people. If I'm sending pages to the set, or they've done a big, tough scene and they've got it in their heads, and then they get changes that night, I think that's bad showrunning. I try to be 48 hours ahead of the train, and not just 24 hours ahead of the train.

SHAWN RYAN, Showrunner: The Shield, The Unit

I give each actor an afternoon to come in to the writers' room to meet with the writers, to hear about the kinds of stories we have in mind for the show, the kind of arcs we have in mind for their character. We ask the actor a lot of questions. "What do you think your character would do in this situation? If your character got stuck, you know, between here and here, which way do you think they'd go?" We hear their answers, we engage with them, make them part of the process.

If they have an idea, we don't always use it, but we certainly engage them in a creative partnership because a character is a joint creation between those of us who write it and those people that play it. I find if you include them there, if you give them a script on time, if they know that there's an open-door policy, if you have a question or something that you either A) don't get or B) disagree with even, here's the time period to talk to us about that. That time period is not when the cameras are ready to film and the whole crew is waiting for the work to get done; it's before that.

Those rare times when you've done all that and yet you're getting the call that says, "Hey, the cameras aren't rolling and this or that," that's when you know you have to take it as an individual case. And that's why the scripts have to be so good when they go out, because you have to be able to defend every single line and every single scene. You need to be able to answer every single question to them and, essentially when an actor has a problem, I find that it's usually because they're fearful that they're going to look bad. There's something in the writing of that scene that makes them either secretly think, "I don't know how to play this and therefore I'm gonna come off in a non-flattering way," or "There's something about the scene that I don't understand and therefore I can't play it." Sometimes it's a matter of talking through the scene in a way that they can understand it. It's also a thing where you need to build trust.

I had that on *The Shield*. I had an actor, like, get upset four or five times and really question the storyline we were doing, saying, "You can't do this on TV!" I said, "Well we're going to do it and here's why..." I still got some resistance, but I got them to do it and then when this person saw the pilot and saw the episodes that came out, it was like, "Oh I see what you're after, I get it. I don't know why I didn't think of it that way." It's a matter of explaining it to them, and fortunately I haven't been in too many positions where I've got actors storming off set and refusing to come out of trailers, but I've heard plenty of stories about that as well. Ultimately, the writers want the show to look good and actors want to look good in those shows, and if you can find that middle point where the writing will be good and the actor will look good, then everyone's happy.

RUNNING MULTIPLE SERIES

In this era of modern television, showrunners with successful shows become brands: David Chase, J.J. Abrams, Shonda Rhimes, Joss Whedon. These writers are so successful at creating hit TV shows that their names alone bring immediate eyes to a series because of a built-in fan base. So when studios and networks are developing new shows, the industry leans towards brand names because they want to be in business with existing success. What that creates is a TV landscape with successful showrunners guiding a lot of shows, because their concepts get picked up.

Does that mean they are actually showrunning multiple series all at once? Often, yes. In some cases, a showrunner may run the writers' room and let the day-to-day of everything else go to a co-showrunner or executive producer. Or they might lean on their writers' staff for story arc and episode outlines, and they come in for clean-up or script revisions and post-production. There are a lot of different options to create the right paradigm, but let's face it, one show is exhausting enough. How do some showrunners actively lead more than one series at a time?

Joss Whedon

❝ The year I had three shows… I had a lot of focus. I don't know if you saw *Limitless* with Bradley Cooper? That was like me, but I didn't have those piercing eyes. I had [showrunner] David Greenwalt very suddenly leave *Angel* and [*Buffy* showrunner] Marti Noxon, not quite as suddenly if I had been paying attention, have a baby. It was basically down to me and [executive producer] Tim Minear. Jeff Bell stepped up [on *Angel*] and everybody else stepped up and we got through it.

"There was one episode of *Angel* that I didn't break that year, that I didn't actually do the story for, that I just gave them a few notes on. Apart from that, 56 episodes, I did them all and it was ridiculously draining. My son was born three days before we finished shooting the last episode of *Firefly*. I don't want to do that again, but it was also an extraordinary time. There was grandeur to it because it was the last year of *Buffy*, so I couldn't drop the ball there. It was the first year of *Firefly*, so I couldn't drop the ball there. It was the fourth year of *Angel* , so I just thought, 'Everybody *knows* that I'm going to drop the ball here, so I can't drop the ball here because that's where they will be looking for it.' There is an element of once you get them all spinning, they kind of balance a little bit. But only for a certain amount of time and then you die of extreme old age. ❞

Shawn Ryan

❝ You've gotta be able to compartmentalize. For a while I was doing two shows at once: *The Shield* and *The Unit*. People would always ask, 'How can you do that?' and I said, 'Well it's actually easier for me. It allows me to not think about *The Shield* for a few hours.' I go over to *The Unit* and I think about that, I deal with these problems and then I get a break from that. You've got to be able to turn on and off.

"I did an interview once where they wanted to see what a typical day was for me on *The Shield* and I came in and I realized going through it that I was doing something on eight different episodes that day.

"We were breaking the story on one episode, I was editing another episode, we were casting on one, we were prepping on another, I was listening to a sound mix from the first episode of the season. I was doing notes on a script that they had coming out. You've got to be able to have all these things in your head, and you're the final line of defense, because mistakes will be made if you don't catch them, and so you have to view that as a challenge. You have to embrace that or everything is going to fly off the cliff. **"**

When Your Show Fails

Succeeding in television is actually an abnormality. The majority of scripts written don't get developed, most pilots don't get picked up, and the majority of series don't succeed past their first season. That means writers need to figure out how to process and get beyond failure even when it hurts. Instead of feeling like a loser because your show wasn't embraced, writers need to learn the lessons of that misstep and apply them to the next attempt. The following are some high-profile television shows that were cancelled, and their showrunners speak frankly about what went wrong and what they learned.

CARNIVALE : 2003–2005, Two Seasons, HBO

RONALD D. MOORE, Showrunner

It was difficult to run a room with a lot of people that [had been] showrunners. It wasn't really terrifying, it was just hard to herd the cattle, you know? It was hard to get everybody on the same page because they all had their own ideas. I don't know if I ever didn't feel like I was running it, but the difficulties of running that particular room had more to do with the fact that half of them hated the other half. Getting them to work together and to not break out in open warfare when you put them in rooms was the biggest challenge. That was a difficult skill set: to sit down to try to talk to them individually, to try to get them to play nice, to try to get some spirit of camaraderie going in the room was something that I never cracked.

The biggest failure of the show, for me, was that I never was able to really get it into an "us" mode. Traditionally, in shows I'd been on, it was always us against the world in the writers' room. Here we are in the bunker, and out there, all the people were trying to shoot at us, and kill us, and trying to hurt us, but all of us sitting around here, around this table or in these chairs, drinking bad soda and chips and ruining our health, we're tight, right? We've got each other's back. That was the first time that didn't happen.

I found it very difficult to navigate the waters between myself and the creator, who didn't run the show because he didn't have the experience as a showrunner. I don't know if I handled it the best way that it could have been handled. It was the first time either one of us had been in that situation, and it was just a hard thing. Here's the man that created the show, it was born on his computer, and you want to defer to that at some level, but you've also got to run the show and it's your responsibility to get it made week-to-week. If you don't think his idea is right, you're the one that is ultimately held responsible for it, so you have to go with what you think is right. That's set up to create friction. I think, at that point in my career, I was probably not ready to handle that situation. I probably could have handled it better. I know he could have handled it better. It just wasn't a great mix.

DIRT : 2007-2008, TWO SEASONS, FX

MATTHEW CARNAHAN, SHOWRUNNER

Working on *Dirt* was all kinds of things. It was a difficult experience. It was an enlightening experience. It was the first time I really feel like I got to have that great feeling of you're making an independent movie, while writing a novel, while painting a painting, which is showrunning at its absolute. But Courtney Cox's character wasn't even in the script when I wrote it. It was a very clear, clean Faust story between an actor who was morally challenged and who was not having success. It was somebody famous and a paparazzo who was basically offering him, in exchange for his soul, favorable media coverage. The FX network president, John Landgraf, really wanted a female-driven series, so I created this kind of Bonnie Fuller-esque character, Lucy Spiller, for Courtney. So in a way my original vision was compromised from the time I said "okay." From there, it both got more interesting and it deteriorated.

If I wanted to continue making my creative thing, I had to address their commercial thing. This is the crucifixion of doing this thing that we're obviously overpaid for and overpraised for. It was ultimately an incredibly difficult and really rewarding creative process. I feel like the pilot I got to make was amazingly cool. The first season I got to make was really cool. The second season [Landgraf] just said, "This is what we're going to do." And I feel like it wasn't so good. And after the second episode, the [WGA] strike happened, and then I had to walk away. I've never seen the second season of *Dirt*, nor do I want to.

That experience definitely caused me to step back and take a look at what I was doing, and how I was doing it. It made me really realize that one simple decision, one simple action, can change the course of your creative endeavor. And I decided I'm never going to say yes in some unconscious way again to anything, when it has to do with work I'm making. If I say yes, it'll be carefully considered. If I sell out, I'll know I'm selling out. And if I say no, I'll have given it the benefit of some serious introspection.

CAPRICA : 2009–2010, One Season, SyFy

JANE ESPENSON, Showrunner

Any problems that had to do with *Caprica* were entirely my fault. I was not prepared to be a showrunner. It's a really hard job, and I hadn't had any particular training for it, because I'd decided from early in my career that the parts of this job that I love are the parts you do least when you're a showrunner. The thing I love is being given an episode that's been broken by a room so I know the structure has been thoroughly vetted, and then going home and just pouring my heart into making those scenes sing as much as I can. And I've since discovered other bits that I love, like being in the editing room and working on how we maximize what we captured on film to make it the best version of what we can build. Love that. I love working with the actors and figuring out if there's an interpretation that they have, something they've thought of that I haven't.

Love all of that, but I didn't know how to do it, and I didn't know how to ask the right questions so I could learn how to do it. I think I bumbled my way through *Caprica* and was very unhappy. I was surrounded by people trying to help me: an amazing writing staff, a fantastic cast and crew who turned in amazing footage that made it look like I knew what I was doing, when I didn't— just fantastic people all around. But I was over my head. And I think it was very good for the show that at a certain point I sort of said, "I'm not getting to do what I love, and you're not loving what I'm doing, that I'm trying to bumble my way through." And so Kevin Murphy and I traded jobs. It was like, "I will be the co-executive producer if you be the EP now." He immediately stepped in and took charge and I was able to just be like, "Ok. Yes. Ok, I see now right away a couple of the mistakes I was making." He did a fantastic job taking the show to the end of its run.

I'm proud of the show. I learned a lot. Everyone else learned a lot. We all came out wiser. Showrunning is incredibly, brutally hard. And you can't really lean on anyone, because part of the job is being the broad shoulders of the show. And there are many women who do it really well. Just in saying that, it makes it sound like I'm saying it's a man's job. No. It's just a job for a really confident person who has a handle on all the different moving parts that make up a show. I really only had a handle on those parts that I adore.

When *Husbands* came along, it was almost like when people talk about, "And then, after all those years of dating and thinking I'd never get married, then my husband came along!" It's like that. This is a show that Brad Bell and I came up with together. We created it. We built it from the ground up, wrote every minute of it, and shot every minute of it. And I wasn't terrified. Doing it this way, having a strong partner, I wasn't in over my head. And so there is something about you finding the right project, the right sized project, the right team, and the right kind of project for you.

THE CHICAGO CODE : 2011, One Season, NBC
TERRIERS : 2010, One Season, FX

SHAWN RYAN, Executive Producer

Both *The Chicago Code* and *Terriers* being canceled was hard in that I thought we made good shows with both. You know, I get that if you make something that isn't good it's going to fail. The hard thing about Hollywood is that good things can fail too, and sometimes bad things can succeed. But I knew in my heart when *The Shield* was wrapping up in the middle of all its critical acclaim, I knew that not everything would go that way. For me, I was like, *The Shield* kind of gives me permission to fail at this point, and fail I did! (*Laughs*)

Ted Griffin, who is a friend of mine, created *Terriers*, and the two of us together—with, once again, a great writing staff and a great team, great actors— we made the show I'm extraordinarily proud of. That's 13 episodes that I would be thrilled for my grandchildren to see some day. I'll stand by those episodes forever.

The Chicago Code, I'm really proud of that show, and showing off Chicago. I'm from the Chicago area and to show off that city in a way and to talk about those issues and to tell those stories… I've no regrets at all about the shows that we made. I regret that we couldn't bring a bigger audience.

I feel bad for my partners at the studios and network, who presumably lost money in those endeavors. It's not like I don't want to care about getting an audience. I just know that audiences are fickle. We had a horrible name for *Terriers*. We could never properly explain to an audience what that show was gonna be, and we couldn't get them to show up to watch it and to fall in love with it, which they may have if they had been enticed to watch it. *The Chicago Code* certainly had its shot when it got a premiere the night after the Super Bowl and got ads during the Super Bowl. I've learned the lesson as a showrunner that you can control the things you can control and unfortunately you can't control 300 million people and what channel they turn the dial to every night.

Yes, self doubt creeps in, not about my ability to make what I think a good show is, but whether my tastes are aligning up to America's tastes. You start thinking about that, and you start thinking: am I doing the right kind of show, am I on the right kind of network, am I casting it in the right way? I feel I have an ability to execute a show well, but am I choosing the right things to do? So you think about that. I've been thinking, "Can I really distill—in a very easily understandable, cool way—what the show is about that's going to cut through the clutter? And if so, then I'll get to make the kind of show I want to make?" I'll be able to do things around the edges, but I've got to make sure that that one, core, cool, succinct idea can come through, because we live in a 500-channel universe. There are just too many options to be something kind of vague that people don't understand, and that was a really huge lesson I learned from *Terriers*.

SWINGTOWN : 2008, ONE SEASON, CBS

MIKE KELLEY, SHOWRUNNER

It's always difficult when you don't have success out of all the hard work. It's funny, I've said a number of times that we could be working just as hard and having no one watch the show. That happens to a lot of people and it did to me. Sometimes it has nothing to do with the quality of the show, but it could be the marriage of the outlet, the network, whether they are on cable. For *Swingtown*, for example, it was more of a cable show that was trying to make it on a network that was not known for drama, certainly not based on people's sex lives.

I also loved the way that *Swingtown* worked out for CBS because, for me, that show was never supposed to be a graphic exploration of how many people you can cram into a bed. It was just meant to be sort of *The Wonder Years* and it was about my childhood. I didn't mind that there were limits working on CBS. I actually felt like it helped me tell the stories I really wanted to tell from memories. I guess that the fact that it never found an audience—it found an audience that loved it, but it didn't find a broad audience—was because it wasn't really meant to. It's a very specific show for a very specific audience. Yes, that hurts. I guess you find a way to be proud of your work and you can stand by it and, at least for me, that rationale that it's special and it remains special for the people that loved it and for the actors and for myself and the rest of the writers that got to produce it. It's going to be something that's special because it was short. The fact that we were able to do really good work is what keeps you moving into your next project.

VIVA LAUGHLIN: 2007, Two Episodes, CBS

STEVEN S. DeKNIGHT, Showrunner: Spartacus

I had a very odd experience on the ill-fated *Viva Laughlin*, the Hugh Jackman musical that was on for about two seconds. Literally, the show premieres right after *CSI* on a special Thursday-night CBS premiere. We lost 10 million viewers from our lead-in, and then we had our second episode that Sunday in our regular scheduled time slot. As I was driving into work on Monday, I got the call that we were canceled.

I ran that show with a great writer, Tyler Bensinger. We both came on as co-executives. The pilot had already been shot, so we were working on the first season, and the show was unfortunately in massive trouble. We really loved the idea of a musical in a Dennis Potter-type, *Pennies from Heaven*, *The Singing Detective* type of musical. We saw the show just falling into absolute ruin. The plug was going to be pulled, so we did the unthinkable. It was your classic Hollywood [moment], we had to go to the studio and say, "Look, we think it's really in trouble and there needs to be a change made." I remember leaving that meeting feeling horrible because we both really loved the showrunner at the time, but it just wasn't working, on any level. We left that meeting with the Sony executives, thinking, "Well, we're either running the show or we just got fired." And the next day, they called up and said, "Okay, you're running the show. Fix it." And at that point, I wish I had been fired.

We went in with the intention of trying to take over the show and attempt to save it. It was a sinking ship on a biblical level. I'd been involved in some tough shows but I'd never been involved in a show that on every single level was becoming a disaster. *Viva Laughlin* has become a bit of a television Hollywood punch line, but that experience of taking over a show that was so deeply troubled, I've got to say, I think I've learned more during that experience than I have in any other experience. It was a crash course of what to do and what not to do.

MEN OF A CERTAIN AGE: 2009–2011, Two Seasons, TNT

MIKE ROYCE, Showrunner

On the day we got canceled, I got the phone call about one in the afternoon on a Friday. I could already see it was leaking out. They called me and then they were going to call Ray [Romano]. I also called Ray. He was doing a charity golf tournament on television. I turn on my TV and there he is, walking blissfully down the fairway, and I'm trying to get a hold of him. I know he's got his cell in his pocket. I'm just worried that people are going to come up to him and go, "Hey, your show just got canceled." It was horrible because I couldn't talk to anybody before I told him, obviously. Finally after this excruciating time of an hour or two, I'm watching him get on the phone and just maintaining a poker face as I talk to him. That was brutal.

I would say my feelings about TNT are very complicated, only because I did understand. I was not in a position to go, "Look at these numbers, what are you crazy?" At the same time, I and a lot of people at TNT as well, felt this show deserved renewal. It was scheduled in a crazy way. People are trying their best, so it's not like people went, "Let's kill this show." Quite the opposite. Everybody was trying their best. Promotion was extraordinary. There were so many commercials. We were the big thing to promote besides *The Closer*. It was really hard for me to complain about what TNT did. They took a show that was a stretch for their brand. They really tried to expand and I think they're doing a very good job expanding their brand. This was a show that I think a lot of people who watch TNT said, "This is not the kind of show I want to see on TNT." It didn't mean the show was bad, but if you look at the other TNT shows, it's just not the same kind of show.

I think *Friday Night Lights* got caught in this as well. I think there's a lot of shows that if you have a quiet, naturalistic show, certainly dialog-driven, no giant events, no cops, no emergency medical procedures, it's an uphill battle on broadcast television. For that matter, TNT is a very broad cable network. They're trying to appeal to a very broad audience. I have to hand it to them for never interfering, never. Letting us do the show that we wanted and then trying to promote it in the best way they could. I was disappointed only because we were all disappointed. I know they were disappointed. This wasn't a case of, "We told you guys this wouldn't work, so fuck you." It was quite the opposite. We were getting a lot of critical acclaim. They can't have hated that. I think we did a very good job with the show. I just think it was the combination of being a little too different for the network, combined with scheduling, combined with not as many episodes as we probably should have produced to gain an audience that was going to stay with us.

IN DEPTH:

How *Lost* Changed Showrunning

We all know *Lost* was a landmark television drama because of its cult following, its expansive mysteries, subversive sci-fi storytelling, and groundbreaking social-media audience engagement. But it was also the first show of its kind to propel its showrunners, Damon Lindelof and Carlton Cuse, into the mainstream spotlight, setting a precedent for what a showrunner might be expected to do for the success of their show.

Jeff Melvoin, founder of the WGA Showrunners Training Program, explains that *Lost* helped prove that social media and television integration was the wave of the future.

JEFF MELVOIN

I think some shows are much better suited to a digital presence, to a web presence, than others, but even the most straight-ahead drama—that has no necessarily sophisticated component that would naturally lend itself to social media—needs a social media presence. But there are two things that we have to distinguish here. First is the trend that actually said you have to exploit the Internet in a way that supports the show in a content-related way, and I think *Lost* is probably the best example. *Lost* found itself riding this wave where suddenly they realized people wanted more information. They were very savvy about it, and they began to create all sorts of branded merchandise, not just on the web. Carlton Cuse said, "Sometimes I don't feel like a showrunner, I feel like a brand manager," and I think that was particularly true for *Lost*. They wanted him to do all sorts of things, including webisodes.

I think that, like it or not, since *Lost*, it's simply a fact that part of the job of showrunning now is there's going to be these ancillary responsibilities that the network, or studio, expect to be handled. The thing you have to be careful about is they are still giving us only 24 hours in a day, and if they expect you to be managing that, especially content-related stuff like extra episodes, or little snippets of episodes, it's tremendously debilitating and time consuming. You have to educate the network and the studio that this is not what you're really paying me for. Yes, I can give you webisodes, and then when we shut down, or when the show that we actually put on the air—the mothership—isn't any good I can tell you why: because I've been taking your notes on webisodes.

As a Guild member, and a former Guild board member, I think we have to be very careful about what they're asking us to do with our time and professional ability. If they're saying they want your web presence... so you want me to write? What do you want me to write? What are you going to pay me to write? It is part of your day, and if that's part of your professional responsibility, okay. But I expect to be compensated for it, and I expect you to understand that it's taking time away from other things that I do. I think if you make them understand that, then they're going to put fewer demands on the showrunner to do it.

The question is who is going to be responsible for that web content, and I think that the burden should fall on the studio and/or the network. We [the writers] will give you information. We'll advise you on it, or if you want somebody on my staff to be a liaison, let's create a position. Let's fund it. Let's pay for it, and that person will be the interface, but you cannot expect the creative team, and especially the showrunner, to be doing double duty and creating that presence. There's always exceptions with people who love that stuff. I mean Kurt Sutter has had a lot of fun stirring the pot. Bill Lawrence has gone out on a limb in many ways to promote his show *Cougar Town*, and God bless him. I think it's great. I think Bill would be the first person to say, "I don't want to create a standard that other people are going to have to follow," but fortunately or unfortunately, the effort that he put into trying to promote the show this year by going to different cities, and actually paying for his own promotion, doesn't seem to have helped the cause. I feel bad for him personally, but as he said himself in an interview, "If I succeed, then everybody's going to hate me because now they're going to feel they have to do that."

Damon Lindelof attests to the slippery slope of promotion that came out of his concern that the complicated premise of *Lost* made it necessary to deconstruct the prohibitive elements of the show so more viewers would buy in.

DAMON LINDELOF

I think the decision to become frontmen/our own kind of P.T. Barnums for the show, never felt like a decision that we actually sat down and contemplated. Had it been, I don't think we would have chosen to do that. I think it was more something that just kind of happened to us. J.J. and I were certainly experiencing that when people watched the pilot, across the board, they all had the same reaction, which is, "This is pretty cool, I like this." But how is the show going to sustain itself? What's the next episode going to be? You can't just have the monster chasing these people through the jungle every week. It just feels too complex and too intricate for us to track. So as a result of that being the criticism, it almost forced us into a defensive posture where we had to start going out into the media and saying, "Here's what we're actually going to do. We have these flashback ideas, and it's going to be very character-centric." People would say, "Is the show going to be weird? Is it supernatural?" And we'd say, "No, it's not that supernatural."

Obviously, that evolved over time, but in a lot of ways, we likened it to the idea of after a football game the coach has to put himself in front of the press and explain why the team lost the game, or why the team won the game when, in fact, arbitrarily, he's just the coach. The team has a mind of its own. There was this demand for us to constantly get out and explain things, and we felt like if we denied our audience, if we basically said, "Sorry. The show speaks for itself and we're not going to talk about the show at all," that actually would have hurt the show. And so by making ourselves available, ultimately sometimes to criticism as well as praise or questions or anything, we felt that that was in the best interest of the show.

That evolved to where, by the end of the first season of the show, Carlton and I were asked to do a special that would air before the finale which, basically, recapped the entire season, where we explained, "Here are all the things that you need to know in order to enjoy the finale." So suddenly, I'm just a writer who occasionally does interviews with the press and then I turn on ABC, and there's my ugly bald head trying to explain what the Black Rock is. And Carlton and I just turned to each other and said, "How the hell did this happen?"

Carlton and I have a very interesting dynamic. Carlton is the glass-half-full guy, and I'm the glass-half-empty guy. I always looked at doing anything on-camera as a chore, and it was taking our attention away from where it should be, which was actually working on the show itself. But over time I was convinced that it was a necessary part of the job, going out there and saying, "Hey, we stand by our work."

CHAPTER SIX

THE RISE OF THE SHOWRUNNER

Connecting to the Matrix

side from "showrunner" being a term that's new to the mainstream television lexicon, the idea of a showrunner being embraced as a "celebrity" by its fanbase is a concept writers themselves are still grappling with. While there are plenty of showrunners who love being the public voice for their show—and the praise and adulation that can come with it—there are many who have always preferred the traditional anonymity of a writer weaving their stories off the radar.

If you're a showrunner today, the comfort of staying in the shadows has disappeared. With social-media integration a tremendous part of television marketing, from Twitter to Facebook, tvtag to podcasting, showrunners are expected to help lead the awareness charge for their shows and forge bonds in the cyber-verse with their audiences. Writers' rooms live-tweet episodes in the US for east- and west-coast airings, showrunner post-mortem interviews with major online publications are standard after major episodes, and network websites feature exclusive video content with writers answering fan questions about their shows.

Since the start of the new millennium, to the networks and studios, talking publicly *about* your show is a job requirement as important as writing it, whether a showrunner likes it or not. "The first taste I actually got of that was on *Buffy The Vampire Slayer*," *Spartacus* showrunner Steven S. DeKnight says of when he first realized the shift. "I've always said I owe everything to Joss Whedon. He plucked me from obscurity, taught me how to be a showrunner, and taught me how to be a better writer. But on that show I had my first realization that the writers were treated by the fans in the same regard as the actors, which was something I had never heard of in my life. But everybody realized that Joss' vision for the show, the language of the show, and what he was doing, was so unique that people became fascinated with the people that were actually writing the words. Ever since then I have done my best to interact with the fans."

It's that "interacting with fans" part that becomes a slippery slope for so many showrunners and writers reticent to let themselves be sucked into the fan slipstream. Sure, love and adoration for you and your show is awesome, but if you've spent any time on the Internet following the pop-culture dialogue, then you know the warm-fuzzies can get ugly, real quick.

Back when anonymity was acceptable for showrunners and writers, storyline feedback was limited to television critics' columns in newspapers or magazines, fan letters sent to the office, or a perusal of messageboards focused on their shows. It was a quaint distance that, at times, provided showrunners with some unexpected perspective, or even modest course-correcting, but their creative circle remained insulated and protected.

Now fans have incredible, immediate access to showrunners via Twitter, Facebook, television festivals, and convention appearances, where interaction and candid opinion sharing is completely unfettered. Really dedicated television fans, who thrive on interacting with like-minded viewers on Tumblr and Twitter, develop deep bonds and passionate points of view about how they think they want their shows to unspool. When writers fail to provide that, today's audiences aren't shy about expressing just how disappointed or angry they are about the travesties in writing they have to witness week-to-week. Depending on how deep they allow themselves to go in the cyber world, showrunners can be inundated in real time by unhappy viewers who demand changes, threaten to stop watching, or make comments ranging from the petty to outright terrifying. If there's anything a writer tries to avoid at all costs it is being forced to be creative by committee. If they are constantly trying to temper that reality from happening with people who actually cut their paychecks, it's easy to see why fan interaction with relentlessly negative commenters telling them how suck they are at their job, and how to do it right, might get off-putting.

What is the right balance of interaction, and should showrunners listen to their audience to write their story? Our showrunners talk about how they transitioned into the process of "talking" to their fans, and how to reach a happy middle.

FAN FEEDBACK

JOSS WHEDON, SHOWRUNNER: BUFFY THE VAMPIRE SLAYER, FIREFLY, DOLLHOUSE

I was very lucky in timing. When I started out the idea of an Internet community was a very, very fresh idea. So, the fact that [fans] were able to band together in way that they never had, and I was able to wade into the middle of that and so were my writers, and, when they wanted to, my actors—that was a new phenomenon. To be able to write and have people appreciate what you're doing is a dream. To be able to have them recognize you and be able to speak to you about it, is more than a writer usually gets. That was fortuitous. It created a rapport between me and the fans that I wouldn't have been able to have otherwise. As that's grown, I've distanced myself from it to an extent because I find the business of self-promotion becomes a job. For some people, it's a perfectly legitimate job.

JAMES DUFF, SHOWRUNNER: THE CLOSER, MAJOR CRIMES

One of the things that we've really worked very hard to do is include our audience. The people who watch the show we think of as part of *The Closer* community. We feel like we had a community with our show, which goes back to when I was a kid and I wasn't just watching a television program, I was a part of a community that watched that program. We would talk about it the next day at school. We organized ourselves sometimes around it. I think the community that goes with the show is important, especially nowadays when the public is so fractured and the business model is in disarray. Tending to the audience is a very important thing. They expect certain things, and we're going to give them that.

KURT SUTTER, SHOWRUNNER: SONS OF ANARCHY

I think it's important for me to feel like I'm an author and a motherfucker in terms of vision and sticking to it. I have a very specific point of view about my show, but I'm also very aware that I'm not doing it in a vacuum; that it is a product of the commitment of hundreds of people and that I'm doing it for an audience and we are being financed through advertising. I'm aware of all those things in the mix, because you have to be. I'd be an idiot not to. I'm very aware that this is for the audience. As I write and create things in the show, more often than not I'll take the story in a direction that I know will be incredibly satisfying for the fanbase and for me.

That's one of the reasons why I like things that are a little more pulpy, because they are very entertaining and satisfying. Along with storylines that are more subtle and perhaps more nuanced, there's a component of the show that is just right in your fucking face, and I think I'm aware of that because I know the fans enjoy that. It's important for me that people are aware of that; that I'm not sitting up in my office with the door shut and saying I don't give a fuck about the audience, as people in my position sometimes do.

STEVEN S. DEKNIGHT, Showrunner: Spartacus

My writers' room is always telling me to stop looking at the Internet. Very rarely do I interact with the very negative criticism, but sometimes there's something so egregious that I just have to comment. And I've gotten into a dust-up twice now that I can think of where I found out later I was actually in a yelling match with like a 12-year-old, which is always surprising when that happens.

But I haven't found it gets in the way of the job. It just makes you a slightly bigger target because when things go bad, when people don't agree with what you're doing, or think you have ruined what they considered their show, and rightly so, they can now show up electronically with torches ready to burn the place down. I've seen this happen to showrunners that I desperately respect. I think it happened to Damon [Lindelof] on *Lost*. I think it happened a bit to Ron Moore at the end of *Battlestar*. When people disagree with you, and they have a forum openly where they can all get together and disagree together, it can be a frightful thing. For a showrunner, it's a bit of a neurotic thing, you know. I spend way too much time on the Internet seeing what people think, which is also a bit odd, because the way we work, our shows are completely shot before they're ever aired, so they're complaints about the show I can't do anything about.

JANET TAMARO, Showrunner: Rizzoli & Isles

It hurts my feelings when people say mean things. But I think that is true of all writers. We're sensitive. That's part of why we're writers—and what makes us good. It also makes us vulnerable to criticism. A creative endeavor is a difficult thing, but when you do it, and put it out there, you will get feedback. I don't expect everyone to stand up and applaud, but I remember reading a particularly nasty review and thinking, "You know, when you do your first show, I'll be happy to review it." Thanks to social media, any yutz with a smartphone can "publish," despite the fact that the content may not be any different from what was scribbled on a bathroom wall back in the day. But it's now instantly internationally available.

I do myself a favor most of the time, and I don't look at it. But I read reviews of all shows when they debut. It's encouraging to read critics who I respect, who understand what it is I'm trying to do or what another writer is trying to do. It helps to mitigate the comments from those who didn't seem to get it, and make nasty comments—that's my perspective—maybe they're brilliant, incisive comments. But I accept that I've put myself out there. Nine million people are watching. If you're going to come into this crazy kitchen, you better be ready for the heat.

RONALD D. MOORE, Showrunner: Battlestar Galactica, Outlander

Well, the online community and fandom in general has a certain proprietary sense of any property that they're involved with. The *Star Trek* fans certainly felt that way. The *Star Wars* fans definitely feel that way, and so do the *Battlestar* fans—both of the old show and of my show. I can't really cater to them, because you know it's not a poll-driven process. It's not a democratic process. I don't turn to them for input of what they want or what they would like. I go with what I think is the best story. Criticism kind of goes along with the job. People are free to say what they think about it, whether they like it or not.

Ultimately it's probably good that people have access to the person or persons that really can supply most of the answers, who can give insight in the creative process and explain why certain creative choices were made, why certain choices were not made, and to give you the inside story, because ultimately that's really what fandom craves. I mean, when I was a fan of *Star Trek* growing up, I wanted to know why Gene Roddenberry did certain things or why Gene L. Coon did certain things as a writer/producer.

JOHN ROGERS, Showrunner: Leverage, The Librarians

I would say that what you are doing is trying to create a core audience that will also proselytize for you. There is just so much background noise. There is so much media and entertainment. I don't think anyone is trying to grow anything; we're just trying to survive. What you're trying to do is say, "Hey, people that I know out there that like this like I do, we're on! Please, over here. You'll dig it, if you just watch." Once they come, they go, "Oh. Yeah, I do like it. I didn't even know this was on." You're just trying to punch through that noise. What you're really trying to do is, maybe over the course of three years or four years, I think the outreach we've done over that amount of time has given us a base that keeps us from bleeding under in the off season, and then slowly builds as they tell their friends and it legitimizes the show.

CHRIS DOWNEY, Showrunner: Leverage

We haven't had monster ratings on this show, but our feeling is that the people that watch the show really, really like it. They are into it. Those people want more content. They want more interaction with the show. They want to feel like they belong to the show. I think that has been a part of why we've grown every year. We've kept this core audience, and every season we've added to that. Our show is about a team of thieves and grifters and hackers who help the little guy.

We had a *Leverage* convention where we met people face-to-face. People friend us on Facebook... I've gotten really heartbreaking stories from people looking for *Leverage* to help them in this sticky situation they have at work or with their family. You have to put some distance.

DAMON LINDELOF, SHOWRUNNER: LOST, THE LEFTOVERS

The audience would ask us, "Are you making it up as you go along?" and they wanted the answer to be no. But then they would ask us another question, which is, "How much does fan input matter? Are you listening to us?" They wanted the answer to that question to be yes. What the audience didn't realize is, these two questions are at direct odds with each other. You want us to have a plan that is totally fixed and that we never deviate from, but you also want us to listen to you. So, how can we do both? That was an enormously interesting conversation that we were having with the audience as it flowed, but I do feel that the lesson learned—and all the showrunners whose writing I really follow and appreciate seem to do it this way—is that they are very open to the idea of changing the plan if inspiration strikes, or if the original plan is not working. The worst thing that you could possibly do is, once the ship starts sinking, you don't change your plan.

Any writer who cares about what they're writing and says that they don't care what the audience thinks is– I'm not saying that they're lying; it's just not something that I can relate to. Why would I be doing this unless I cared what the audience thought? I have respect for a guy like J. D. Salinger who wrote his books and then he put them in a trunk and he locked them up. That's not caring what the audience thinks, that's just being a writer. But if I'm going to write something and I'm going to make it, and put it on television, then, yes, I'm going to care what the audience thinks. You take it personally when an idea that you are trying to convey, or an emotional theme, or any of your storytelling is not connecting, or people are saying things to you like, "You wasted the last six years of my life," or, "You're a horrible person," or, "You're a liar." You take those things personally.

HART HANSON, Showrunner: Bones, The Finder, Backstrom

I pay no attention at all, because the people who complain about such things are not our usual, standard audience. Our job is to manipulate your emotions, so it's funny that the loud people get mad at you for that and it's actually what they're tuning in for. I think 99.85 percent of the audience is not thinking about what I'm doing to them. They're watching the show and they don't know my name, they don't know that people write it even.

My father was on set once and he was watching Brennan [Emily Deschanel]. My dad has watched TV since they've made TV. He loves it. First time he saw my name on TV, he had a little weep (and he's a logger, he's not a weepy guy). He was standing watching Emily say one of her scientific things, something I'd written, and he turned to me and said, "Wow. How did she come up with that stuff?" That's my dad. That's the audience: those people who don't know how the soup is made. There's a very small portion of the audience that thinks they know how the soup is made and give you advice on how much salt to put in it. I think they should be ignored because it's not that they're stupid or anything—ok, some of them are stupid, some of them are very, very smart—but you should ignore it because they're not your audience. You're working for someone else.

SHOWRUNNERS AS CELEBS

I t used to be that the only celebrities of television were the actors who were featured in the shows. Maybe the industry itself lauded big-name producers, or a few game-changing creators like Aaron Spelling or Norman Lear would rise to household-name stature, but overall the face of your show was your cast.

Not anymore.

With the rise of the showrunner, the creators and writers of pop culture, buzz-worthy shows are getting lots of face time on red carpets and interview shows. Unless an executive producer has purposefully made the transition from acting to writing/producing, it's still an odd by-product for many writers who aren't comfortable with the spotlight. Many eventually warm to it and can be as charming and entertaining as their cast members, but others admit they have to dig deep to thwart their introverted tendencies.

DAVID SHORE, Showrunner: House

I think it's great in theory that people are paying so much attention to writers in the form of showrunners. I think recognition of what writers contribute to the process is overdue and fantastic. One of the reasons I like watching the Emmys more than the Oscars is that everybody gets up on stage at the Emmys and thanks the writers and everybody gets up on stage at the Oscars and thanks the director. Having said that, I prefer to be a little more anonymous; I like my privacy. I like to have a real life, so I don't want to be famous. It is nice when people recognize my name and tell me how much they love the show. That's very nice, but it's nice in limited doses. I've been out in public with Hugh Laurie and I wouldn't want to live that life. I haven't hired a publicist. I have no intention of hiring a publicist.

JANE ESPENSON, Showrunner: Caprica, Husbands

It is insane and wonderful that writers now are sometimes treated with the same reverence that the actors get, particularly in sci-fi. Sci-fi fans understand that the ideas are important, and that the ideas are generated by the writers. DVD commentary and conventions have given them the chance to actually know and recognize our faces. Amazing. I never anticipated that. The notion that some kid in Omaha is seeing [a commentary] and going, "Oh, Jane Espenson wrote a joke I like," and then connects to me on Twitter and talks with me about their life… Fantastic! We are in a gilded age.

STEVEN S. DeKNIGHT

The thing that the Internet has really changed is that it puts creators and showrunners at the forefront. I think that it, together with things like DVDs with the extras and the interviews and the commentaries, has really moved the people behind the scenes in front of the camera. The pinnacle of that, of course, being Damon Lindelof and Carlton Cuse doing their periodic ABC specials explaining what's going on in *Lost*, which I think is a great thing. I'd like to see more of that. I know growing up as a kid, the showrunner name that I was most familiar with particularly was Stephen J. Cannell, and really that was because of his company card at the end. It's still burned into my mind—him at his typewriter, he throws the sheet of paper, and then his logo comes up. That was really my first introduction to the notion that somebody actually creates these. Somebody writes these. Somebody loses sleep over making this television that I love.

I think there's absolutely more branding of showrunners these days. I often tell all of my writers in the room that in this day and age you can't just be in the writing business. If you're in it, you've got to think of yourself as one of the commodities. You really gotta put yourself out there, sell yourself, and once you have brand recognition that will go a long way to get you help to get done what you need to have done. It is great in this day and age for a showrunner. There's gotta be a bit of P.T. Barnum about it. You've really got to sell yourself and your product, and by doing that you create a buzz in Hollywood and among the studios and the networks that kind of goes, "Oh, yeah, I've heard of this guy. I've seen this guy. I like his interviews. Let's get this guy in and talk about this project. Let's see what he has to say."

Is Twitter a Writer's Friend or Foe?

I n social-media circles, Twitter is the undisputed hub for showrunner interaction with fans. Many of the big executive producers have an account, and they interact in varying degrees with their audience. Networks often push their showrunners and cast to tweet, especially during the first year of a show when strong digital engagement can translate to better ratings or DVR-viewing stats. But aside from marketing, what's the upside to being a vocal showrunner on Twitter? Can it be an actual tool to help further their careers? What do they get from engaging with the audience directly?

HART HANSON, SHOWRUNNER: BONES, THE FINDER, BACKSTROM

I got onto Twitter because Stephen Fry was on our show *Bones*, and kept talking about the importance of social media. Of course there was Myspace and Facebook, but Twitter actually showed me what it was. It's fascinating, so I thought, "Oh, I should do that." I wanted to see what it was all about. I've kind of rued the day ever since. Twitter is another place to popularize or publicize your show, so I gave it a shot. Certainly, because I was on Twitter, and I was one of the first showrunners to be on Twitter, I think, or in the first 50 to be on Twitter, I was mentioned, and our show was mentioned, in a few print articles that we might otherwise not have been mentioned in.

To this day, I still don't know what it does for us, if it's good or bad, or if it has any effect at all. If I offended every single person who followed me on Twitter, and they never watched my show again, it wouldn't be a drop in the ratings. It wouldn't register, unless, for some reason, a whole bunch of them had Nielsen boxes. I can't tell. I don't have a feel for it. I don't look at the Hart Hanson page to see what people are saying to me. They either think I'm the second coming of

Jesus Christ, which I'm not, or they just hate my guts. Neither one of those things are particularly interesting, or helpful, to me, or the show.

JANE ESPENSON, SHOWRUNNER: CAPRICA, HUSBANDS

I love Twitter. I feel like I was born to tweet. Is it essential for communicating with the fans? Kind of, yeah. It's certainly good for letting people get a sense of my character. I think it's important not to become a short-order cook. Not to be listening to what the fans are saying they want to see, and cooking it up and delivering it to them. I got something that was like, "Look at this, here's a link to a great idea for a storyline you can do on *Once Upon a Time*." Those things are toxic. The last thing you want to do is either find yourself falling into someone else's rabbit hole of story idea or be accused of having done so, which would be terrible. You certainly don't want to end up writing a story that's not your story, that's not your passion.

I think Twitter could be kinda dangerous. It gives you a little too much access into every moment of what the fans are thinking. If the writers of *Cheers* had had Twitter, they would've been besieged by people going, "Get Sam and Diane together." Sometimes what the fans [think they] want is different than what they really want. What you want is that tension of, "here's the thing that I want and I'm not quite getting it yet." You want the delayed gratification. You just don't know that's what you want. You can tell when the fans are tracking the story. You can tell when they're confused. You don't want confused fans. You can tell when they're bored. You don't want bored fans. So, it does give you a way to take the temperature.

DAVID SHORE, SHOWRUNNER: HOUSE

It's tough to avoid it. Even if you're never online, I hear comments about what people are saying online. I try to avoid it because it depresses me, because it's just people saying what an idiot David Shore is. That's what it feels like to me. It's like going to a dinner party with 10,000 people who each have an opinion on your work. As valid as every one of those opinions may be, it's very difficult to sit there and listen to that. I also circle back to my basic opinion: "I've got to do a show that I like." That's all that ultimately counts. I'm not saying I deserve to be on the air. I only deserve to be on the air if people like it, but I ultimately have to do a show that I like.

I recognize it's important for the publicity for the show and to get viewership on the show, but I resent it on a certain level because I just want the episodes to speak for themselves. So when inside people start commenting, I think it changes the viewing experience or it has the potential to do that. I create a story. You watch that story. Take from it what you want and, hopefully, you'll enjoy it.

KURT SUTTER, SHOWRUNNER: SONS OF ANARCHY

I'm trying a lot of different things, obviously, through Twitter and Facebook and my blog. It really began through the blog, which was a complete experiment for me. That's really what started the ball rolling for me, and then, obviously, Facebook and Twitter. But it is important to me. It's fascinating to be able to have that instantaneous, one-on-one with the fans. In my case, it's sometimes very dangerous, because I'm a rather impulsive and opinionated guy and it has come back to bite me in the ass on more than a few occasions. John Solberg, our FX PR guy—I've just given that guy so much agita over the last couple years with all that. He gets very nervous, but I think they've learned that it's a specific point of view, and that the truth is it's freedom of speech and they really can't control that. Now, if I was libeling myself or I was libeling them I'm sure it would then fall into a legal issue, but I'm really not. It's totally my opinion and my experience, and I don't think it's hurt the show in any capacity. I think if anything it's perhaps at least given people awareness of the show and perhaps allowed them to take a peek at it. I'm very careful about not doing anything that, A) gets me fired, or B) puts them in a compromising position. I don't want to spoil anything for the fans. Trust me, there have been a good 15 or 20 blogs that I never published because ultimately I felt like it would have compromised them and made it difficult for them, and that's not the purpose of that.

[Bloggers] will do full reviews of individual episodes now. I've stopped reading those because I feel like sometimes the critics get bored in the process and I've found some of those to be sort of mean-spirited or not really indicative of the show itself, or the show as a whole. I didn't find reading those useful. They were more distracting than anything. Of course, I will read reviews when the first four episodes go out to critics. More often than not, I'll read reviews where people are reviewing the season as a whole. I never read comments on blogs. I learned very early on that there's just a lot of angry fucking people out there. I don't do that. I have a friend of mine who was in my employ that does that religiously and, God bless him, I just can't do it.

In terms of [social media's] value and the importance, I don't know if there's a clock or a meter to measure that. My concern, and it was our concern on *The Shield* and our concern with this show to a certain extent, is that we only do 13 episodes. There's almost an eight- or nine-month period between seasons, which is a long time to ask people to stay excited about the show. With social media, I'm allowed to at least plug back into the fans and tell them about what's going on.

SHAWN RYAN, SHOWRUNNER: THE SHIELD, THE UNIT

I think there's value in it, in that a lot of TV critics follow me, and I follow other TV showrunners on Twitter. We make critics aware through our tweeting of things that are coming up in episodes, reminding them about things. I don't have a study to prove it, but the critics will write more about the stuff that you're tweeting about than if you are silent about your show, and so therefore maybe there's some more press along that way.

There are TV executives who work in networks and studios that I'm associated with who follow me, and you know, that maybe keeps me and my projects on their radar a little bit more. I think it would be effective in that regard. I think there are some super fans of these shows who follow you and 90 percent of the tweets you get about your show come from the same 20 people who want to talk about it, and if those people talk a lot about it you don't know what kind of cascading effect it has. So I think it has an effect, but it's a self-serving ego thing if I'm honest, about those of us who work behind the camera who are mostly anonymous to people. Our names are kind of known, but who we are isn't really known, and here's a chance to kind of express a little bit of who we are. We think we have an impact on what these shows are and yet, we're relatively anonymous.

MIKE ROYCE, SHOWRUNNER: MEN OF A CERTAIN AGE, ENLISTED

The bad thing about Twitter is that it's a distraction when you're writing. The good thing is when you're about to kill yourself, you could let everybody know.

[When *Men of a Certain Age* was canceled] there was a group of fans who decided to try and save the show. It gathered a lot of steam. Ray [Romano] and I were trying to sell the show to another network, and TNT was, to their credit, not stopping us. The fans really started this whole big movement, mostly through this Facebook page that was sort of a headquarters. I actually ended up reaching out to a few of them, which I wasn't sure whether to do because you're not sure who you're dealing with. It was amazing because they were just people: a mom, a businessman, just people who loved the show. They made it their mission to try and do whatever they could to bring it back. They didn't know anything about economics, or television, or how anything worked; it was this group of four or five who just worked hours and hours a day to try and make it happen. There's one guy who messaged me named Leo. About every two weeks I get a message like, "I just watched this episode again for the eleventh time." And then he brings up some new thing that he hasn't brought up before. He just really connected with it. It's very touching. To have this level of people just relating to what we were doing and feeling this loss, it really was like we lost a friend. It's so self-aggrandizing to talk about show business this way. It's show business, I get it. Artistically, it just felt like this giant loss. That certainly doesn't happen with every show. I think this group of people felt the same way.

ENDING A SERIES

T here's an interesting new paradigm when it comes to bringing a television series to a close these days. If a showrunner is given the opportunity to bring a show to its natural, narrative end, they run the risk of jeopardizing their entire reputation on that series based on whether or not they stick the landing of their finale.

It's certainly not the fairest bellwether of success, especially when it can be documented critically and statistically that the majority of episodes that came before the end might have been lauded as excellent quality. But that doesn't really matter anymore it seems, because there's an odd fascination with critics and audiences who pin the success or failure of a series finale as the determinant of the show's entire worth. Some of it comes from the controversial endings of *The Sopranos* and *Lost*, which ended up being very subjective codas that enraged or confused a good portion of their audiences.

Fans who felt betrayed by those high-profile endings seem to now want a creator/showrunner to know exactly how they're going to end the story from the pilot, as if that will somehow merit total clarity. And if that pre-determined end is still found lacking, well, you better run! Yes, there's not a lot of sense in any of it, but when it comes to passionate fandoms, it's about the gut, not the process. And for the showrunner, all it boils down to is being more aware that their already sweat-inducing last hurrah for the series is going to be that much harder to write.

DAVID SHORE, SHOWRUNNER: HOUSE

It's a tricky thing with the lifespan of a TV show. At a certain point, shows get tired, it's inevitable. You do your best. But *House* is a show about a human life, and I really never viewed it as a show with a beginning, middle, and end. Perhaps because I never imagined it going so long, I never really imagined that there would even be an option to end it on my terms. I just always assumed at a certain point it would just go away because I would run out of stories or people would stop watching. That's the tricky thing about it. More to the point, the quality of the show depends on the quality of the execution more than the big idea. That applies to episodes and it applies to a series.

Endings of a series are tough to do. Aside from *Newhart*, I can't think of one show that had an ending that everybody was really excited about. No, that's not true, *Mary Tyler Moore* had it. It's wonderful when you come up with a truly original idea, but generally speaking, you are doing ideas that have been done before, and that's ok. It's how you execute it. It's what you bring to that story, what new insight you bring to that story.

JOHN ROGERS, SHOWRUNNER: LEVERAGE, THE LIBRARIANS

It is interesting because we actually wrote every season as if it could be the last one. We actually made sure the last episode of every season, if that was the last episode of *Leverage* that you ever see, that it was a wrap up. We said, "If we are only going to make these thirteen, we are going to make the hell out of it!" And that's why I like the micro-ending! I like the idea that we told that story for that year well. I hate cliffhangers. I hate cliffhangers with a burning passion. Come back and watch our show. We're not going to give you the really cool part of the episode; you've got to come back next week. Screw you. Give the people their ending and come up with some new shit next year. Give the people their fucking ending.

KURT SUTTER, SHOWRUNNER: SONS OF ANARCHY

I feel like in terms of the *Lost* situation, I saw that coming. I just knew that the build for the ending of that show began about three years [into it] and that there was no way those guys were going to be able to do something that satisfied everybody. The fact was that they had a very specific point of view, they wrote toward it, and they wrote what they believed was the best way to end the show. On *The Shield* we took a big risk in terms of how we ended with Vic Mackey [Michael Chiklis]. He didn't go out with a bang; he went out with a whimper. Creatively that was a bit of a risk for us to do, but we felt like we earned it, and that it was the most fitting way for that character to end, to sort of slip into purgatory.

I'm sure, as I get to the end of [*Sons of Anarchy*], following the path that I'm going on, there will be people that will be very satisfied and people that will want my fucking head on a plate. I'm aware that the reactions can be big and that they're out there.

J.H. WYMAN'S GUIDELINES FOR ENDING A SERIES

When co-showrunner Jeff Pinkner departed *Fringe* before the show's fifth and final season, J.H. Wyman was left to navigate the last season alone. *Fringe* wasn't created with a concrete ending in mind, so Wyman was left to ponder how to end the show. Having witnessed the blowback around *Lost*'s finale, a fellow Bad Robot series, Wyman explains how he had to merge what he envisioned with what the fans expected.

J.H. Wyman

❝ Nobody wants to tell a story that people don't enjoy. I think with *Lost*, I admired Damon tremendously. He gave people years and years of incredible television and changed the landscape of what we understand as good drama on television, and look at the thanks he gets. In the very wise words of my good friend, Gore Verbinski, he said, 'It's not a pizza. You don't get to order it the way you want.' That's how I feel about Damon. He did what he felt was right. As an artist, I'm going, 'Great. That was cool. If you believe in that, then I'm with you.' I feel like people can feel whatever they want, but you can't get upset because it doesn't go the way that you wanted it to.

"[With *Fringe*] I was thinking, 'How am I going to end this? What's important? There's a million little things that need to be tied up, but what are the ones that are really crucial?' I went away and I started to think about it, and I said, 'What would I want?' I'm a huge fan of television. What would I expect? Truthfully, that's the only way that I could come to an answer that I could understand and live with and accept.

"Here are my criteria: I would want everything to make sense. I've invested so many years of my life watching and falling in love with these characters, and I would really love to understand that the journey I was taking was for a reason; that the characters would find themselves in positions and ends that we may not expect, but which are logical and moving. I would demand that.

"On the other hand, and this was probably the most difficult, I would like to watch it as a fan, and I would like to have an incredible feeling of, 'Oh my gosh, that was so moving and perfect!' The next day when I got up, I would like to get in my car to go to work, and I'd like to be able to think of the characters that I loved so much, and I imagine where they would be, and be able to have the concept that their lives went on, and that they're not gone, they're not too far away.

"By the time I finished that script and then shot it, and put my name on it, I can guarantee that I stand behind it

100 percent. If they don't like it, there's nobody to blame but myself, and that's fine. Really, the satisfaction for me is getting to tell these incredible stories. I'm very fortunate that somebody pays me to do art, but at the end of the day, it's my art. I'm trying to say something with pictures and images, and if someone doesn't like the way I say it, that's okay. They're entitled to their opinion. It took a long time for me to learn that, to be okay with that. **"**

DAMON LINDELOF

We knew that, "Oh my God. There are going to be a lot of people who don't like the ending." We had this very profound realization that the same year we decided we were going to do our endpoint was the year that *The Sopranos* finale aired. Carlton and I both watched *The Sopranos* finale. We were in New York at the time and we were just completely blown away by how awesome *The Sopranos* finale was. The next morning we got up, we started talking about it and then we went into this room with all these other people. We were like, "Did you see *The Sopranos* finale last night?" They were like, "Yeah, wasn't it a cop-out?" We looked at each other and said, "We're fucked." Because despite this idea that it doesn't matter what you do in the ending, the fact that the show itself is ending creates this entirely new emotional response. Not to say that a TV show is like a person, but it is like a relationship. The functioning metaphor became death.

If you know someone is dying, you're going to have one or two reactions. One is you get really close to them and you're like, "I'm going to appreciate every minute I have left with this person. I love them so much." The other emotional response is, "I cannot become attached to this person anymore because they're going to die, and I'm very sad about that. Therefore, I don't like this person." That's kind of what happened with our show.

ANDREW MARLOWE

I have a great ending for [*Castle*]. It's that Bob Newhart wakes up in bed next to Suzanne Pleshette and the whole thing has been a dream. No, I don't have a specific ending in mind for *Castle* because I feel like these characters are very much alive to me and we're dealing with a living, breathing relationship. Relationships are complicated. In a lot of ways relationships never end. You can get married to your wife and then after 30 years there are things that you're still finding and growing, and challenges that you're still having. So I haven't come up with a beautiful ending for the show yet, but I don't feel yet that I've had to.

There are many ways to end the show. Do you end it with a wedding or a funeral? Or do you end it with something else entirely? Is there a version of it where Castle and Beckett open their own detective agency and then you're spinning off another show? We're just not there yet. We have a lot of storytelling left and it may be that the clock runs out at the network and studio before we've gotten to the end of their relationship, in which case we'll probably figure out a way to go out that's graceful for where those characters are in that moment in their relationship.

JAMES DUFF, SHOWRUNNER: THE CLOSER, MAJOR CRIMES

I did have the opportunity to end the story the way I wanted to, which is something that you don't always get in television. Sometimes the audience stops watching and off you go, and you don't know what your last episode is going to be. I'd known that we were going to be ending our show for a long time, and I knew what I wanted the last show to be, and I've always known what I wanted the last show to be. I'd been thinking about the last show since I wrote the pilot, and I felt like I'd been taking the journey towards that last show from the very beginning. I can tell you I ended the show the way I expected to end it, and that I believe it's the right way to end the show, and that I think that it's the right way for the character to exit, and I feel in my heart that I have done the best I could do

.

RONALD D. MOORE

The [*Battlestar Galactica*] finale took some flak from some of the people in the online fandom. I kind of expected that. I don't really care about that. I'm happy with the finale. To me, that's the end of the story and people are free to like it or dislike it, but that is the end of the story. That's the complete tale that we told. There's not another version, the alternate ending floating around in my head that makes me go, "Oh, I wish I'd done that." That's the ending that I chose and that's the ending that I think the story deserved and I think the characters deserved.

You know, the criticism will go away also. You tend to watch these things rise and fall over time. I remember when the finale of *MASH* aired, which had one of the biggest television audiences in history up to that point, it took a huge amount of flak for the ending. People just lambasted it the next day and people grumbled about it for years and years, but over the course of time people now look fondly at it. Now it's like, "Oh yeah, remember when Hawkeye thought that he was strangling a chicken and it was actually a child, and what a brilliant thing that was and how sweet and bitter-sweet."

DAMON LINDELOF

At the end of the day, as cheesy as it sounds, it really all comes down to this idea of, what's your relationship with the material? Was the ending the ending that we wanted to do? How do we feel about it? It's nice that there are some fans out there who say, "It touched me. It was really beautiful," but in the same way that you can't let the fans who say that they hated it really get to you, or affect your own relationship with the material, it's the same both ways.

Walking Away from Your Show

When a writer gets the opportunity to create a show and then executive produce it, the outcome is going to turn out one of three ways. One, the show won't make it, and the mythology or end-game for the show will never get the chance to be filmed for audiences to get story closure. It's a common outcome, and one that emotionally tackles both the storyteller and the viewer.

Two, the showrunner will guide the series through a number of successful years, and either by their own choice, or the studio or network's choice, will move on and hand the creative reins over to another executive producer. In the best-case scenarios, the showrunner will have developed a new show to foster and move forward creatively, signaling it as the natural time to leave their show in the capable hands of another. However, in other cases, a showrunner might not get the chance to finish the show on their terms and they walk away, leaving everyone, especially dedicated viewers, always wondering how the series "should" have ended, like it went down with *Gilmore Girls* after Amy Sherman-Palladino's departure.

Lastly, there are the showrunners who get their show idea birthed and commit to seeing the story through all the way to the last fade to black. These lifer showrunners often had a very clear arc in mind from the inception of the idea, and consider the seasons to be like chapters of a book. They wouldn't dream of leaving the book unfinished.

Every showrunner has to come to their own crossroads and decide whether to stay or go, for their own personal reasons. Here they discuss their own choices.

DEE JOHNSON, Showrunner: Boss, Nashville

There is always trepidation when you come into an existing show. There wasn't a full personnel change [at *Boss*], but when there is a personnel change you always have to wonder how you are going to fare. But the difference is there is a template. So the expectations are large but at the same time I'm not here to reinvent the wheel. I'm here to take a fantastic show and carry the torch. It's obviously daunting to some degree, but since I'm not looking to reinvent the wheel, I don't look at it as a problem. I think it's a good thing.

CHRIS DOWNEY, SHOWRUNNER: LEVERAGE

It used to be that you'd get the show up until you wanted to put a gun in your mouth and then you would find these magical showrunners who would come in—who we like to call them hospice workers—who would kind of like feed the show and give it pain-relieving medicine. It's palliative care for your show as the life ebbs from it and then it dies. There was a whole group of showrunners who did this. And, meanwhile, that was making money for the original show creators who moved on to an island and what-have-you. And now there's a lot more cradle-to-grave, like David Chase with *The Sopranos* and Phil Rosenthal with *Everybody Loves Raymond*. These guys took their shows from beginning to end and they didn't want another voice.

JOHN ROGERS, SHOWRUNNER: LEVERAGE, THE LIBRARIANS

The agents in particular are usually the first ones to notice things, because they're the most aggressive and terrifying. They began to realize that the shows that do better are the ones with that guy or those guys staying. I think it's such a crowded media space that shows need something special to survive, and a lot of it is not necessarily that person's talent but that person's love. It's that person's commitment. It's not just a job. It's the thing we made happen and now we will ride this out. You're also looking at a sea change where, five, six years for a show now is a long run. Most TV shows don't get past that anymore.

HART HANSON, SHOWRUNNER: BONES, THE FINDER, BACKSTROM

I get really itchy after about three seasons. I've never worked on a show as long as I've worked on *Bones*, even ones I've created. You get a bit itchy. Also, I have an overall deal with 20th [Century TV], the studio, and I'm supposed to provide them with a pilot each year, so I've done that with varying degrees of enthusiasm. It just feels like part of my contract. Sometimes they want things and sometimes they don't. I felt I owed it to myself and to the studio to have the next thing there.

RONALD D. MOORE, SHOWRUNNER: BATTLESTAR GALACTICA, OUTLANDER

In the third season [of *Roswell*] Jason [Katims] stepped away. He had some development to go do and so he handed me the show in the third season to pretty much run. It went from The WB TV network to UPN, and that was difficult but exciting at the same time. It was a positive experience at UPN. They weren't quite as difficult as the people with The WB were, creatively. However, the ratings didn't earn us a fourth season.

GREG PLAGEMAN, SHOWRUNNER: PERSON OF INTEREST

I think the part that intrigues us is the serialized aspect of the show, building that out. If we feel like we get to a point where it's run its course there, we'd probably get tired of it. Other than that, we can go indefinitely.

JONATHAN NOLAN, SHOWRUNNER: PERSON OF INTEREST

The franchise of our show is inexhaustible. New York is never going to run out of crime, sadly. So, that case-of-the-week is positioned more in the *Law and Order* school of: do you have 20 seasons in you? I don't. Sorry, spoiler alert. (*Laughs*)

THE FUTURE

With the television-producing landscape frantically adapting and morphing to keep up with the speed of rapidly shifting technology, the only certainty in the industry is that there will still be programming. Where it's viewed, who pays for it, and how the system will function for everyone in the business of making television, and those of us watching it, remains up in the air.

"I'm not sure it's going to settle down ever, at least in the future that we can predict," showrunner Jeff Melvoin theorizes. "I think there will always be broadcast cable, and broadcast television in some form. If there is, CBS will be the last man standing because they know what they're doing, and they do it great. But the range of shows that's out there, and the definition of what makes a successful show, is changing quite a bit. Having grown up with *The Ed Sullivan Show*, for example, I think there's something sad, or at least something that you can get wistful about, when a show could draw 60/70 million people to it and the whole country could be talking about it the next day."

Those days are certainly long gone, because of DVRs, the Internet, and a myriad of other entertainment distractions. Content consumers now spend huge parts of their entertainment time on their tablets, smart phones, and laptops. The Internet is the new hub provider of content, and some showrunners are chasing the broadband route as the delivery medium of choice. Streaming providers like Netflix are taking advantage by luring creatives like showrunner Beau Willimon and his political series, *House of Cards*. The show is a critical darling, and according to Netflix's Chief Content Officer Ted Sarandos, a subscriber hit (the service won't release original content metrics). In this new streaming world, that means ratings aren't even a qualifier for success. As Sarandos said at the Hollywood Radio and Television Society's programmers event in 2014, "We're looking for a proportional success." For a television writer that is creative nirvana.

WEB SERIES

n 2008, Joss Whedon became one of the first showrunners to experiment with the Internet as a conduit for original programming. Born out of the WGA writers' strike, and seeing the importance of new media, Whedon created the three-part musical *Dr. Horrible's Sing-Along Blog*. It proved that fans would respond to niche programming that didn't fit on cable or broadcast television, and that a profit could be made. Whedon has yet to create the sequel or return to this exact model of content creation, but he's still experimenting with collaborations with sites like Vimeo, and video on demand, to get his programming right to his fanbase.

JOSS WHEDON

I love the Internet for very different reasons. To put a show on the Internet, the return on that is such that it would have to be something very tiny. There are opportunities to do things that are serialized, but on a smaller scale, that I'm very interested in pursuing. But television is its own thing. One of the things about that that was fun for us, was that we wanted to make a television event in the way that they don't exist anymore. We stream it for free on this day, this day, this day, because, there was a time when it was like, "Ooh, *Lonesome Dove* is on. It's a big deal and this is an important night. We all sit around and watch it." The idea of appointment Internet was really exciting to me because that's what I grew up with. You make the time. You clear the desks, you finish dinner, you rush to the room, you all gather. The fact that that's old fashioned now is hilarious.

The only thing I can say about what's to come is that there's going to be a hilarious series of misfires, because right now what the Internet is capable of providing is growing. What TV is capable of holding onto is shrinking, but they haven't met in the middle in any significant way. I think ultimately what we're going to see is both entrenching and reaching. The idea of a TV season has already sort of disappeared. Things just start and stop when they do, and then people find them the ways that they do. I think we'll be able to take some more chances in certain ways because the [concept of] 22 episodes—it's got to be this order, and you get 100 of them, and then you get syndication—that's all changing, which frees up the networks a little bit to say, "Well, let's try something a little funkier."

At the same time, they'll want to batten down the hatches and churn out the most dead-headed sitcom they possibly can. Not in the brilliant dead-head fashion, but in the having people's heads being dead. They'll want to churn out just pap to make sure that people keep coming for that kind of thing. I think it's less difficult for original voices to break out in TV than it ever has been. It's still hard. Everybody who has a show that worked, and maybe it's the first show they ever created, they're going to tell you the horror that it was getting that first show on the air.

JANE ESPENSON

When we started [the web series] *Husbands*, my first thought was: we put this up on the web, we demonstrate there's an audience for this, and then TV will want it. Now I realize, why would we want to go there when we've demonstrated there's an audience for it right where it is? We can do it in a way where we don't have bosses saying how we do it. We can do it in the way the consumer most wants it, get it directly to them, and they can help us fund it. Why wouldn't TV end and this new thing start? It's not just that the connection between the creator and the viewer is more direct; it's that the line between creator and viewer disappears. I'm both the viewer and the creator. They're both the viewer and the creator. Sponsors can get involved because their products are both paying for and are featured in all of the same bits of entertainment. Now there's money in this circle so it can keep going. It's really going to turn into something quite wonderful, I think. It's happening as we speak; every week the medium is changing.

Is Scripted Programming in Trouble?

Producer, screenwriter, and former actor Dean Devlin knows the entertainment business inside and out. He's made blockbuster films from *Independence Day* to *The Patriot*, figured out how to scale down the adventure genre to TV-budget size with the successful TNT *The Librarian* films, and helped make *Leverage* a five-season hit. Despite his successes, he's worried about the state of scripted programming in an industry that's changing too fast to value what writers bring to the table.

Dean Devlin

" It's the Wild West right now. Scripted entertainment is on the ropes, and anyone who thinks it isn't is not paying attention. It's really difficult to do scripted entertainment right now. The economics favor reality TV, so anything that allows us ways to create an ecosystem that makes it sensible to make entertainment is fantastic. Netflix opening up is like a new HBO; it's another place that you can sell a show or make money.

"Traditionally if you were to finance a TV series you could make a lot of money out of foreign sales, you made a lot of money off the DVD and other ancillary rights, and then you had a huge sale if you made it to five years because you would have enough episodes to go into syndication and secondary markets. Well, today almost all of those revenue streams have dried up, so, in that case, how do you make a business out of it? I welcome anything like Netflix that helps to support the ecosystem.

"If you look at the demographics right now, no one under 30 watches TV. If you look at those same demographics, no one over 30 goes to movies unless they're bringing their kids to see something, so that's a frightening trend. That means TV might have been a fad that lasted only 70 years—I mean that's a scary idea. And it's even scarier if you're making feature films. If the world's going to turn to video games and reality shows that will be a sad loss for people who care about scripted entertainment. That's why there's this huge effort to find new ways to reach the audience, to communicate with the audience, to monetize this, to fight piracy. We may go down, but we won't go down without a fight! **"**

A Showrunner's Path

With the industry in such flux, writers are also trying to navigate the best paths for their creative careers. Is broadcast in too much disarray to invest? Is cable the right fit for future development? Maybe TV needs to get its act together, and film is the place to hang out for a while? All showrunners are mulling these options, and more, as they think about what their personal futures hold.

ROBERT KING, Showrunner: The Good Wife

Would we consider going to cable for the next show? Yes! Because, even though we like the self-contained aspect of network, what we love about network is that you're shooting one as you're writing the next, or the next one after that, so there's a real organic quality to the way these shows grow. In cable, you usually write them all, film them all, write them all, film them all. What seems advantageous about cable is raising a family, actually engaging with your family more than the three or four weeks a year that you're on hiatus. There is something that seems very livable, and also, it seems much more approximate to a novel, the serialized novel, which we love.

ANDREW MARLOWE, Showrunner: Castle

A lot of people ask me, "Do you want to continue in television or would you rather go back to features?" I say, "Can't I do both?" There's something really fun about features where you walk onto a set and you see the 150 million dollars that you've been spending for that two hours. There's something about creating that experience in the temple that is the movie theater where you can really deal with heightened emotions and go into huge worlds in a really interesting way.

But there's also something to be said about the day-to-day storytelling and being able to develop your characters over three, four, five, six, seven years. They're both really great mediums, so even though their base DNA in terms of the storytelling are the same, they require different skill sets, different muscles, and accomplish different things, and I'm interested in both.

DAVID SHORE, SHOWRUNNER: HOUSE

I probably will go back into TV. It's been good to me, as TV has been to writers generally. We get to be in charge. We get to tell our stories and we get to tell multiple stories. I think I did something well [with *House*], but I got lucky. A lot of things came together here. *House* is very personal. I don't expect to match this. The success has floored me. I can't imagine it. It's not why I do it. I just want to get as big an audience as I can to stay on the air, but this has been unbelievable.

HART HANSON, SHOWRUNNER: BONES, THE FINDER, BACKSTROM

You know, here's what's going to happen. I'm old. One day, no one will call me. No one will want me to be a showrunner. They just statistically won't want that, so that's when I'll stop being a showrunner, and then the question will be, will I go write a book or will I go do cable? Will I go work for one of the people who have come up past me? I don't know the answer to any of those things because right now I really cannot see past Christmas.

BILL PRADY, SHOWRUNNER: THE BIG BANG THEORY

Personally, for me, after *The Big Bang Theory* (which is I think my fifth or sixth television series) I don't know if series television is where I would want to tell stories. Series television is an odd intersection of creative work and factory work in that you have to keep making them. It may be a younger man's game. I don't know if there are any monarchies opening up, but I've always thought ruling a nation would be an interesting line of work. I don't know how you transition from what I'm doing now to that, but I'm interested.

STEVEN S. DeKNIGHT, Showrunner: Spartacus

Ten years from now I would love to follow the path of a J.J. Abrams, who I think sets a great career goal for anybody who is a showrunner, which is to get to a level where you can have multiple shows on television, where you can co-create shows with the writers you've worked with, and love, and you can also have a feature career. I think that is the ideal thing to shoot for and he's someone that I definitely look up to, not only a creative level, but as a business model. I think that is the thing that every showrunner should shoot for: to have that kind of breadth and depth to your creations.

At one point early on in my career—I think everybody faces it at some point—I was worried that I had run out of ideas. I had nothing left. I had no new projects planned, and I thought: well, what if that's it, what if the well is dry? Eleven years later, I'm faced with the opposite problem, which is that I have so many projects up on my project board that I look at them and realize there is no way I can do all these before the Grim Reaper takes me. I'm going to go tits up before I get all this stuff out there and I started thinking, "Well, there's nothing to say that I have to do all of this." But for me I think the best thing at this point in my career is to try to use the success to do another show, maybe a couple of shows, but get to the point where I can co-create shows with people, help them get it off the ground, come in every now and then and give some encouraging words and lob a few grenades and then ska-doodle.

The Crystal Ball

Right now, no one knows how the TV industry is going to shake out, but the showrunners certainly see the writing on the wall. They know change is here by necessity, but there's no consensus on what topic is going to dismantle the house of cards first, or what might put the industry right. Gratefully, despite frustration, the showrunners express a lot of hope for their art expanding and flourishing, even with a lot of bumps to come.

JAMES DUFF, SHOWRUNNER: THE CLOSER, MAJOR CRIMES

First off, let's talk about what television is. Television is a monetized delivery system for home entertainment. It is nothing else. It is not format. It is not network. It is not story. It is a mechanism. How that mechanism works in the future is going to be impacted by how technology changes everything. I think the television business right now is 100 percent up for grabs.

I urge you, go downtown to a Tower Records in downtown Hollywood or Beverly Hills; it's gone. Virgin Records, gone. Also, many of the major bookstore chains are gone. I predict, in the not-too-distant future, that networks will also be gone. They are unaffordable, for the most part. Creative destruction is always a little bit bizarre and we don't know how we'll come out of it, but I am a content provider, as they call it, a writer, and people will still want a story. People always want a story, so the people who are telling stories, I think, have a good chance to survive the coming wave. But the wave is coming. We are like dinosaurs regarding the meteor from afar. The meteor is coming. Some people are planning for the next evolutionary process and some people are just eating tree leaves as fast as they can.

MIKE ROYCE, Showrunner: Men of a Certain Age, Enlisted

My feeling on the future of television, which should be taken with whatever the biggest grain of salt you have is, is that anybody who says television is dead is an idiot and anyone who says television is fine is an idiot, so there are a lot of idiots. It's all a slow progression of things migrating to other technologies, but people always like to watch shows. People always like to be entertained. That's all just changing and it's changing slowly.

It doesn't mean show business is over. That goes for television, too. Television is just this thing now where it's a box that has many different ways of getting entertainment to you. That's already changed. Netflix is making shows. Amazon is making shows. That's great. That's all awesome. There are a million cable networks. As far as the broadcast networks go, the ratings are going down every year, but mystically I find that around the upfronts the revenue seems to be awesome. Right around the union negotiations television begins to be dying. The role of the storyteller, however that manifests itself, through whatever technology is happening, is always absolutely going to be there.

JANE ESPENSON, Showrunner: Caprica, Husbands

I think television has a huge future, we just may not call it television anymore. It's got to merge with the computer; it's got to all become one box. Even now I have friends who, when you go to their living room and you look up at their TV, what you see is their computer desktop, and they are using their TV screen as their monitor. We're at the forefront of a new era and it is an era with some really distinct differences from the way TV has been done before.

DEE JOHNSON, Showrunner: Boss, Nashville

I don't know what broadcast is going to do, just because of TiVo alone. I'm just as guilty as the next person of zipping through those commercials, and I don't know how they manage that. It's already changed. My last season of *ER* was season 11, which wasn't that long ago. It was 2005, and at that time we were still getting 23 shares, and that was like waning. There was erosion. Now, that would be a monster hit. It's all sort of cycled down, and I don't know how you then manage with fewer eyeballs, fewer numbers. I don't know.

ANDREW MARLOWE, Showrunner: Castle

Television has become really compelling because it's in a fight for survival. Entertainment has become so diverse when you have the Internet. You have gaming. You have a hundred channels of niche entertainment for the folks who are interested in bass fishing or exploring the Amazon or finding crazy stuff at yard sales. You have a show for each one of those. So, it's fractured the audience in a way that we haven't really seen in our contemporary history. It's always been the big three networks that have controlled everything, and before that a handful of radio stations. So, the culture was all having the same conversation. What's happening now is that we're going to this more specialized, niche programming which has forced conventional broadcast television to become much more competitive. It's forced it to become better just to survive. Your average show that takes place now versus your average show from 20, 30 years ago—the level of storytelling is just much more sophisticated. There are a lot more moves because we're all trying to break through the noise. We're all trying to find an audience and make them think that our hour's worthwhile.

JOHN ROGERS, Showrunner: Leverage, The Librarians

I can't remember who wrote this, but it was a really great writer talking about newspapers, and he said that nobody likes to be alive during the revolution. Before the revolution is cool and after the revolution is cool, not during. We're during right now. Audiences are fragmenting, and nobody can quite figure out how to monetize other delivery systems, but you know what, although I know I occasionally come across as a giant socialist, I am a giant capitalist and I believe the market always figures out a way. At some point, all of this is going to fall out, and we are going to figure out some way. Americans want their scripted television. The world wants their scripted television. Entertainment is the only trade surplus that America has. We buy Chinese furniture, we buy Japanese cars, but the world watches American entertainment. There is some way that this will work out where storytellers can make a living telling their stories. It may only be in half hours, it might be only in 15 minutes, it might be video games, and you'll adapt as long as you as writers are able to go, "Alright, how are you going to let me tell my stories? I've got to learn that set of rules? I'll learn that set of rules."

DEVELOPMENT OVERHAUL

As referenced in chapter one, the pilot system is reinventing itself along with the rest of the industry. Ronald D. Moore sees the antiquated development process as a huge contributing factor to the current economic crunch facing networks. He sees the future evolving from how the system reinvents itself.

Ronald D. Moore
" I think the pilot system is irretrievably broken. I think it is a stupid system, I don't think anyone would ever design production of television to run like this, and the only reason it does is inertia. It was conceived at a very different time. It was conceived at a time when there were only three networks, when the relationship between studios and networks was very different. We have a system that makes no sense economically and creatively. Economically, here are all these studios that produce pilots to the tune of millions of dollars, between five and ten million dollars for a one-hour pilot, depending on who you're doing it for, and what the show is, and so on. You produce this pilot, you spend a month shooting it, a couple of weeks doing post, put it in front of the network, and then they kind of randomly, and I think it *is* kind of randomly, decide,

'We like it,' or 'We don't like it. And if we don't like it, then you, the studio, are out millions of dollars with no way to recoup your investment. Sorry.' Does that make any sense to anybody?

"The people that put up all the money, the millions of dollars the studios put up, have the least amount of power in the process. The networks, who put up the least amount of money, have all the power, and get to say yes or no based on what they think their network brand is and what they think will work on their air, which are questions that they could have figured out way back at the point where you pitched them the concept to begin with. This is a ludicrous process. In my opinion, they should just make shows. They think pilots are really atypical of the series. They're not necessarily the best example of the series, and good series need some time to develop. The famous examples are things like *Seinfeld*. The pilot tested terribly. If you go back and look at the pilot of *Seinfeld*, it doesn't look anything like the series. The series needs time to find its legs. The networks should just say, 'We're going to do a year of the show. We'll stand by it for the first year. We'll feel it out. We'll see what's working and what's not, we'll find its best time slot, we'll work it out creatively, but we'll give it a year,' which is what they used to do in the old days.

"I think cable has a lot of advantages. The fact that they will run the whole season gives them a chance to really find the audience and gives them a chance to actually make the show work over the course of time. The audience is more likely to stick with it because they know it's not likely to disappear next week. And cable allows you to push the boundaries creatively; they can just be richer, darker, more interesting kinds of shows. They can be niche shows; they don't have to appeal to some giant demographic. Cable's got huge advantages over broadcast. I'm not seeing how those advantages go away.

"The networks may not exist in the next five to ten years, but, to be fair, we have been saying that for quite a while now. It hasn't quite happened. I personally think there will be a tipping point where everything changes; you're starting to see that. Netflix is starting to do its own series. AMC was a cable channel that just decided to do original programming. I feel like what I do is secure in that I'm a writer, first and foremost. I'm going to want to write something for somebody, and someone's going to want to make it. I will find someone to distribute things that I like to do in some form. If I was writing for something that was just on the Internet and was performing on something. com, if I'm happy doing it, and I could feed my family, then I'm happy doing that, too. **"**

ALI LeROI, SHOWRUNNER: EVERYBODY HATES CHRIS, ARE WE THERE YET?

I know that there are people who think the future of television is uncertain, and it is, from the standpoint of how certain businesses want to sell it. The thing about television versus films versus the Internet is if you understand that they themselves are not just ways to deliver content, they are actual experiences. The experience that you have when you're watching television tends to be one when you're in some sort of personal space. You have control of it. You have control of the content that's being delivered to you. You want to be able to experience that content in some sort of relaxing fashion, whether that's having a drink, or eating a meal, or sitting down with somebody that you care about. Television can be a shared experience. What's happening on the Internet tends not to be, unless everybody gathers around your phone for 45 seconds, "Hey, guys, look at this." If you understand that people have a desire to have an experience with content, then you understand this delivery system is not going to go away.

Networks are in trouble; studios, not so much. People will pay for television. They'll pay for radio. They'll do all of that, and that entirely screws what networks do. They're struggling to stay in the business of being a middleman between the studios and the audience. "We can get your content out to lots of people in a way that you can't," they say, but that structure is slowly going away. So TV will be here, it's just that there's going to be a lot of people who really didn't do a lot anyway. They're going to be in trouble.

MATTHEW CARNAHAN, Showrunner: House of Lies

I do feel like we're in the middle of a golden age in television. I mean if you put network television aside, which I don't really participate in, and look at what's happening, it's really cool. There's great stuff on the air that I actually want to watch. Not that I am the arbiter of what is good television, but that's all I can really go by. I want to keep making television because it's the only thing other than writing books where you really get to arc out these huge stories and have this kind of leisurely narrative structure. I love it.

HART HANSON, Showrunner: Bones, The Finder, Backstrom

There are so many variables. I cannot see the future of scripted programming, except that I know they always need content. Where it's going to go? What's going to happen to networks? I'm really glad I don't run a network because I'd really be thinking, "Wow, what happens to network TV in a world of cable?" I don't know the answer. Are we going to lose NBC in the next few years? Will one of the giant networks actually go away or will it find itself and what will it be? I don't have any of the answers. My kids do not watch television. They don't own televisions. They don't know anyone who does. If they're going to watch something, they watch it on their computer. No one wants to talk about the fact that the TV audience is aging rapidly. Everyone is going after that demo, but that demo doesn't watch TV. I have no idea what's going to happen. They'll need content for something, but I don't know how you get paid for it. I don't know where it's going to be. I don't know if American TV will continue to be the giant industry it is. I have no idea. Do you?

SHOWRUNNER BIOGRAPHIES

MATTHEW CARNAHAN was the creator/showrunner of *Trinity, Dirt*, and now Showtime's *House of Lies*. A playwright and television writer, Carnahan's first television series, *Trinity*, was executive produced by esteemed showrunner John Wells (*E.R.*).

STEVEN S. DEKNIGHT was the creator/showrunner of *Spartacus* and is now running Marvel's *Daredevil* series on Netflix. A Millville, New Jersey native, DeKnight's first television writing job was on MTV's *Undressed*. He's also written and directed episodes of *Angel, Smallville* and *Dollhouse*. Twitter: @stevendeknight

CHRIS DOWNEY was the co-creator of *Leverage*. Born and raised in New York City, Downey's first television writing job was on *Cosby*. He has also written on *King & Maxwell* and *Almost Human*. Twitter: @ChrDowney

JAMES DUFF was the creator/showrunner of *The Closer* and it's spin-off *Major Crimes*. Hailing from New Orleans, Louisiana, Duff started by writing television movies and his first staff television job was on *Popular*. Twitter: @JamesADuff

JANE ESPENSON was the showrunner for season one of *Caprica* and is co-creator/co-showrunner for *Husbands* with Brad Bell. She is currently a consulting producer on *Once Upon A Time*. Born in Ames, Iowa, Espenson's first television script credit was for *Monty*. Twitter: @JaneEspenson

HART HANSON was the creator/showrunner of *Bones, The Finder* and currently, *Backstrom*. Born in California but raised in Canada, Hanson's first television writing job was on CBC TV's *The Beachcombers*. Twitter: @HartHanson

DEE JOHNSON was the showrunner for *Boss* and she is currently running *Nashville* with Callie Khouri. Johnson's first professional writing job was on the original *Melrose Place*. Twitter: @deemosswood

MIKE KELLEY was the creator/showrunner of *Swingtown* and *Revenge,* stepping down as showrunner on *Revenge* after Season 2. Born and raised in Chicago, Illinois, Kelley's first television writing job was on *Providence*.

ROBERT & MICHELLE KING were the co-creators/showrunners of *In Justice* and currently *The Good Wife*. Robert was a feature writer until he and Michelle teamed up as television writing partners. Robert has also directed six episodes of *The Good Wife*.

ALI LEROI was the co-creator/showrunner of *Everybody Loves Chris* and *Are We There Yet?* LeRoi started in standup and sketch comedy writing, with his first television writing credit on *Comic Justice*. LeRoi also directed many episodes of *Everybody Loves Chris* and *Are We There Yet?* Twitter: @mrleroi

DAMON LINDELOF was the co-creator/co-showrunner of *Lost* and is currently running HBO's *The Leftovers*. Born and raised in Teaneck, New Jersey, Lindelof got his first professional writing credit on *Wasteland*.

ANDREW MARLOWE is the creator of *Castle,* stepping down as showrunner at the end of Season 6. Originally a film screenplay writer (*Air Force One*), Marlowe's first television writing credit was for the series *Viper*. Twitter: @AndrewWMarlowe

JEFF MELVOIN was a showrunner on *Picket Fences* & *Army Wives*. He is also the founder of the WGA Showrunner Training Program. Melvoin's first staff writing position was on *Remington Steele*. Twitter: @Jumper139

RONALD D. MOORE was the showrunner for *Roswell Season 3* and showrunner for *Carnivale*, *Battlestar Galactica*, and currently, *Outlander*. From Chowchilla, California, his first writing job was for *Star Trek: The Next Generation*. Twitter: @RonDMoore

JONATHAN NOLAN is the creator and co-showrunner of *Person of Interest*. Primarily a feature screenwriter with his brother Christopher Nolan (*The Dark Knight*, *Interstellar*), Jonathan's first foray into television is *Person Of Interest*.

JEFF PINKNER was the showrunner for *Alias Season 5* and the co-showrunner of *Fringe*. Hailing from Maryland, Pinkner's first writing credit was for *Ally McBeal*. Twitter: @JPFRINGE

GREG PLAGEMAN is the co-showrunner of *Person of Interest* and was previously co-showrunner on *Cold Case*. A veteran one-hour drama writer, Plageman wrote his first professional television script for the original *Beverly Hills 90210*.

BILL PRADY is the co-creator of *The Big Bang Theory* and was showrunner for

Seasons 1-5. He previously ran *Dharma & Greg*. A Michigan native, Prady started writing for children's television with Jim Henson's Muppets. Outside of the comedy genre he also contributed to an episode of *Star Trek: Voyager*. Twitter: @billprady

JOHN ROGERS was the co-creator/co-showrunner of *Leverage* and currently is showrunner of *The Librarians*. Born in Massachusetts but raised in Canada, Rogers's first television job was on *Cosby*. Rogers also directed four episodes of *Leverage*. Twitter: @jonrog1

MIKE ROYCE was showrunner of *Lucky Louie*, *Men of a Certain Age*, and *Enlisted*. Born in New York, Royce was a standup comedian in New York City and writer on *Saturday Night Live*. His first television series credit is for *Apt. 2F*. He was most recently co-showrunner on *Enlisted* with creator Kevin Biegel Twitter: @MikeRoyce

SHAWN RYAN was the creator/showrunner of *The Shield*, *The Chicago Code*, and co-creator/showrunner of *Last Resort*. From Illinois, Ryan first got into television writing an episode of *My Two Dads*. Twitter: @ShawnRyanTV

DAVID SHORE was the creator/showrunner of *House, M.D.* and is the co-creator of *Battle Creek*. Born and raised in Ontario, Shore started out as a lawyer but turned to writing in the mid-nineties. His first professional script was for *The Hardy Boys*. Twitter: @shorez

KURT SUTTER is the creator/showrunner of *Sons of Anarchy* and upcoming *The Bastard Executioner*. From Rahway, New Jersey, Sutter was an actor and film screenwriter before he turned to television writing with *The Shield*. Sutter directed one episode of *The Shield* and many episodes of *Sons of Anarchy*. Twitter: @sutterink

JANET TAMARO was the developer/showrunner for *Rizzoli & Isles*. Originally a television news reporter, Tamaro changed careers and began writing for television starting with an episode of *Law & Order: Special Victims Unit*. Twitter: @JanetTamaro

JOSS WHEDON was the creator and showrunner of *Buffy the Vampire Slayer*, *Firefly*, and *Dollhouse* and co-creator of *Angel*. Raised in New York, Whedon's first television writing job was on *Roseanne*. Most recently, he co-created and executive produces ABC's *Agents of S.H.I.E.L.D.* and has directed both of Marvel's *Avengers* films. Twitter: @josswhedon

TERENCE WINTER is the creator/showrunner of HBO's *Boardwalk Empire*. Born and bred in New York City, Winter started out as a lawyer but shifted to writing where he got his start on the series, *The Great Defender*. Winter wrote numerous episodes of *The Sopranos* and directed one. He was recently Oscar nominated for his *The Wolf Of Wall Street* screenplay.

J.H. WYMAN was the creator/showrunner of *Keen Eddie* and *Almost Human,* and the co-showrunner of *Fringe*. Born in California but raised in Canada, Wyman was an actor and screenwriter who first ventured into TV writing with CBC's *Wind at My Back*. Twitter: @JHWYMAN

WEBSITE: SHOWRUNNERSTHEMOVIE.COM
TWITTER: @SHOWRUNNERSFILM
FACEBOOK: FACEBOOK.COM/SHOWRUNNERS
YOUTUBE CHANNEL: SHOWRUNNERSFILM

ACKNOWLEDGMENTS

Tara **Bennett** (@TaraDBennett) would like to thank Des Doyle, John Wallace, Ryan P. McGuffey, and the entire *Showrunners* documentary team for entrusting me with the book version of their film. It's been a pleasure and honor to be part of your journey and to shape this project with kindred spirits who love the art of television as much as I do. Also thanks to all of the showrunners who agreed to be part of the book and for sharing such insightful, honest and witty windows into your job.

Thank you to my creative circle who is always there as sounding boards and trusted advisors especially PT for being my collaborator even when the project doesn't have your name on it and Jen H. for giving invaluable early feedback. Thanks to our editor, Simon Ward, and Titan Books for seeing the value in the project and supporting us. My deep admiration also goes out to some showrunners who have been very generous to me over the years including Javier Grillo-Marxuach, Jeff Pinkner, J.H. Wyman, Damon Lindelof, Carlton Cuse, Jane Espenson, Howard Gordon, Bryan Fuller, J.J. Abrams, and Joss Whedon.

And to all of my Rowan University TV writing students who inspire me every semester with their passion for story, for geeking out about great TV, and for digging deep when it comes time to turn their ideas into scripts no matter how hard that journey may be. Your bravery is awesome to watch. One of you name a TV character after me.

Des **Doyle** would like to thank John Wallace, Ryan Patrick McGuffey, Jason Rose (@dcireland), Jimmy Nguyen, and Christof Bove for all of their hard work in helping make *Showrunners*, the film and the book, a reality. Huge thanks also to Tara Bennett for all of her hard work and dedication on this book, and for putting up with me during the writing of it! Her advice, guidance, and encyclopaedic knowledge of TV have been invaluable!

My thanks also to our editor Simon Ward and the team at Titan for helping us make the dream of a companion book become a reality.

To all of the showrunners who have taken part in both the book and the film my heartfelt thanks and gratitude—none of this would have been possible without you. It has been a genuine honour and pleasure to get to meet and talk to all of you.

To all of the showrunners assistants who have helped us during this project, thank you so much—I can't wait to see the shows you guys dream up when you all become showrunners yourselves!

And finally thank you to my family for their unending support, help and belief in me during the making of the film and this book. I wouldn't have made it over the finish line without you!

San Diego Comic Con photography by Jonathan Reilly.
New York Comic Con photography by Bill Edwards

Television Writing Resources

We hope *Showrunners* the film and this book have answered a lot of your questions about writing and creating scripted television. As informative as we hope to be, there's always a lot more to read about the industry. If you aspire to be a writer/ showrunner, then hopefully you are writing, re-writing and reading the various news sites to stay abreast of content trends. Below are some excellent resources that we use often to keep up with the industry or hear from showrunners. These are invaluable for opportunities or insider knowledge.

Network or Studio Writing Fellowships

Disney/ABC Creative Talent Development and Inclusion -
http://www.abctalentdevelopment.com/

Warner Bros Talent Workshop - http://televisionworkshop.warnerbros.com/

Nickelodeon - http://www.nickwriting.com/

CBS Diversity Writing Program -
http://diversity.cbscorporation.com/page.php?id=16

Fox Writers Intensive -
http://www.foxaudiencestrategy.com/fox-writers-intensive/

NBC Writers on the Verge - http://www.nbcunicareers.com/writers-verge

ATX Television Festival Pitch Competition -
http://www.atxfestival.com/programming/pitch/

Writing Resources

Writers' Guild of America, West Resources -
http://www.wga.org/subpage_writersresources.aspx?id=1210

Script Magazine - http://www.scriptmag.com/tv/

Children of Tendu Showrunning Podcast by Javier Grillo-Marxuach and Jose Molina - http://childrenoftendu.libsyn.com/

Nerdist Writer's Panel Podcasts

http://www.nerdist.com/podcast_channel/nerdist-writers-panel-channel/

Showrunner Jeff Lieber's 200+ Rules for Showrunning

http://gointothestory.blcklst.com/showrunner-rules-by-jeff-lieber

Go Into the Story - http://gointothestory.blcklst.com/

10 Excellent Pilot Scripts - http://goodinaroom.com/blog/tv-pilot-scripts/

Ken Levine's Blog - http://kenlevine.blogspot.com/